Getting Unstuck

How to transform your life one step at a time

Cara Stein

Fire Lizard Press

Contents

Don't just get unstuck—
get turbocharged!

Thanks for purchasing this book. I'm super excited for you, and I want to do everything I can to help you. That's why I've included a complete workbook of thought-provoking questions right here in the book. This is your book, so feel free to highlight, take notes, answer questions, and doodle!

But if you're one of those people who just can't stand to write in a book, or if you'd rather type than write, I've also made the workbook downloadable separately. Here's what you'll get:

- 68-page workbook in PDF and Word
- Guiding questions to help you go deeper and apply this book to your unique situation
- Thought-provoking exercises to help you build the life you want
- Step-by-step guidance to help you:
  - Overcome procrastination
  - Figure out what you really want and what you need to do to get it
  - Erase the limits that hold you back
  - Love and support yourself
  - Take action and get results

It's the same questions included here, all in one place, and it's free! You can get it here:

http://17000-days.com/get-turbocharged/

Here's to getting unstuck!

Also by this Author

How to be Happy (No Fairy Dust or Moonbeams Required)
Reclaim Your Love: How to Fix Your Relationship
Relax and Color

Introduction

As you look around at others who are doing what they want and seemingly living the lives of their dreams, you may wonder, why not you? Why do you stay in the same rut, unable to move in any direction, while each birthday brings a reminder that you're no closer to where you want to be? What do those other people know that you don't?

That's what this book is about. To get unstuck, you need to know where you want to go and how to move in that direction. Then you need to start and keep taking action.

When you've tried in the past to change your life, you probably lacked one or many of these essential parts. It's time to bring them all together and break free from what's holding you back.

Why You May be Stuck

Peopleget stuck for many reasons. Perhaps the most common is fear.

We're all afraid of change and uncertainty—we're wired that way. Study after study has shown that people will choose the familiar and the known, even if the alternative is potentially much better. This is why people stay in bad relationships, jobs they hate, houses, towns, careers—you name it. Until the pain of staying becomes greater than the pain of facing uncertainty, we tend to stay put.

We may even leave, only to re-create the same situation in our new circumstances. The pull of the familiar is strong. That's why children of alcoholics tend to choose mates with addictions or substance abuse problems. Even though they see how harmful it is and vow not to follow their childhood patterns into adulthood, those characteristics are undeniably attractive to them, no matter how much they hate them on a conscious level. Why? Because they match their map of the known world.[1]

No matter how much you may hate your job or some parts of your life right now, you know how to get by, right? You know the rules. You know how things work, and you know you can handle it, because you already have been handling it for months or years.

You don't have that confidence about a new situation. You've never been in it before, the rules may be different, you may not know what to do. You may not be able to handle it.

That's one of our biggest fears: that we won't be able to handle whatever happens, whether it's a disaster or just a change. But people are amazingly resilient. We handle everything that happens, one way or another. If you think back over your life, remember the challenges, setbacks, and things that have gone wrong. Some of them were pretty rough, right? Yet you made it through. You handled it. Maybe you found a creative solution to the problem, maybe you fell back on other resources you had put aside, maybe you got help. One way or another, you handled it. You will also find a way to handle anything else that happens from now on.

Another major factor that holds us back is the fear of being wrong or making a bad decision. What if I take the job offer and it turns out I hate it? Or what if I start dating this person and he breaks my heart? We hate the idea that we might make the wrong choice and miss out on something else that would have made us happier. We don't like closing the door on options, and we don't like being wrong. The fear of making a wrong choice keeps many people paralyzed.

Another common factor in staying stuck is simply that change takes effort. The longer we stay in a situation and get comfortable with it, the harder it seems to make a move in another direction. An object at rest stays at rest, and we're no exception.

You may even be combining all of these ideas to form a superglue of stuckness. I've done that plenty of times. For example, when I was working my day job, I wanted to quit for years before I actually did. It wasn't that bad; I just wasn't particularly interested in anything I was doing, and I didn't like the way things were run. But I had it pretty cushy, and what if I quit and liked my new job even less? Or what if I went out on my own, hated that, couldn't make any money at it, and then couldn't get another job when I needed one?

For me, the fear that everything would suck and it would be all my fault for initiating the change was even worse than the fear of not being able to handle it or the fear of making my life worse instead of better. After all, shit happens to everybody, but how foolish would I feel if I pushed away a comfortable situation to choose something that turned out to be a disaster?

Like me, you may wonder what's wrong with you—maybe you've been talking about making a change for years, but never done it. Why do you do this to yourself? Why do you keep putting off something so important to you?

There may be many reasons. It seems counterintuitive, but there are payoffs to staying stuck. One common one is comfort: If you don't change anything, you can stick with the devil you know. Also, you may be getting a lot of attention and sympathy for your situation. It feels cathartic to complain, and it's nice to have people rallying around to comfort you or take your side. Furthermore, as long as you're stuck, you can avoid conflict and pain. Change takes work; being stuck sometimes gets you out of having to make an effort.[2]

In the end, though, fortune favors the bold. You obviously have other things you want to be doing with your life beyond what you're doing now, or you wouldn't have bought this book. What happens next is up to you: you can wake up 30 years from now still doing the exact same thing, or you can start changing your life and sculpting it into what you want it to be.

Think about...

What common themes do your recognize in your life? How do they reflect choices you've made to stick with the familiar?

_____

_____

_____

_____

_____

_____

_____

_____

_____

_____

What change are you hesitating to make?

_____

_____

_____

_____

_____

What are you afraid may go wrong if you make that change?

_____

_____

_____

_____

_____

_____

_____

_____

_____

_____

Which of the payoffs to staying stuck do you recognize in your life?

__ Comfort with the devil you know

__ Attention and sympathy from others

__ The pleasure of complaining

__ Avoiding conflict/pain

__ Not having to make an effort

Unlocking Your Power

Many people share a few internal roadblocks that keep them stuck. As you recognize them and find out how they work, you can go around them.

One common roadblock is the fear of failure, or even just the fear of making mistakes. I think this mindset comes partly from our school days as we were growing up. In class, the teacher tells you the questions and the answers, and then on assignments and tests, if you write the right answer, you're rewarded. If you write the wrong answer, you're marked down. Too many wrong answers and you fail.

After twelve to sixteen years of that (or more!), it's easy to think that's how everything works. You do what you're told, you give the right answer, everything goes well. You don't, you fail.

But life really doesn't work like that. In life, most questions have many possible answers, and often there is no right or wrong. Life is full of trade-offs, and what's best for someone else may not work for you at all.

The first time I started to realize this was a few years ago when I started my yarn-dyeing business. I was really into yarn, and I was

7

excited about the idea of turning a passion into a money-making enterprise. My dream was to be able to support myself with it and quit my job, but even just doing it on the side and making money was an incredibly exciting prospect for me.

But as I bought the supplies and a little bit of equipment to get started, I found myself feeling very anxious. What if I fail? What if this is a completely ridiculous idea, and everyone is laughing at me about it right now, because I just bought several thousand dollars' worth of yarn? What if I'm just indulging my hobby to crazy extremes and this is all an excuse to be an outrageous yarn hoarder? But worst of all, what if the business fails?

I was talking to one of my friends about this, and he pointed out that it's a small business with no employees other than myself. I'm free to try stuff. I can see what works and do more of that, and drop what doesn't. And it's up to me to decide if the business has "failed" or not. As long as I'm willing to keep trying things and working at it, the business will still be running—it's only when I decide not to do it any more that it will end, and if I choose to stop it because something else seems like a better choice, is that really a failure?

This was a totally new outlook for me, and it helped give me the courage to make a serious effort with the business. Ultimately, I burned myself out on yarn. I also concluded that it's too physical to count on for my living. I injured my shoulder, and that made me doubt the wisdom of lifting heavy pots of water and yarn for my livelihood.

However, I still want to get back to doing some dyeing on the side, and I don't consider the whole thing a failure at all. The business knowledge I gained from running the yarn business has been invaluable to me as I've built my writing business and begun to support myself with it. I never could have quit my job less than a year after starting my blog if I hadn't already had the foundation of knowledge and experience from the yarn business. Even though it didn't turn out how I hoped, it was still what I needed.

If you look at your experiences this way, you take failure out of the equation. Things won't always go the way you want, and you'll make decisions that in retrospect seem sub-optimal, but as long as you keep learning and using what you learn to do better, you've never failed. You're just on the path, headed toward what you want. That's a great place to be.

Nobody knows the exact answers or their complete path before they start. If you're doing anything interesting, it's almost guaranteed there is no clear, well-marked path for you to follow. That can make it intimidating: it's easy to spend so much time trying to plan the whole route or trying to find the perfect way to start, that you never start at all.

If you can change your approach and see life as a series of course corrections, you can make it much easier on yourself. Rather than expecting to go directly where you want to go by the shortest, most efficient path, expect to set out in something vaguely resembling the right direction, go a little way, and then re-evaluate. From your new perspective, you'll have a clearer vision of how to get where you're going, so you can adjust your course based on your improved knowledge and set off again.

As you go, you'll keep correcting. You may even realize that you weren't exactly right about where you wanted to go and adjust that, too. That's ok. In fact, it's better than setting a goal and blindly pursuing it even after you realize it's not really what you want any more.

Some people may know what they want right away and never deviate from that, but most of us don't. When I was a little kid, I wanted to be a ballerina, then an artist, then a writer, then a teacher, then a psychologist. When I got to college, I wanted to be a journalist, then the designer who lays out the newspaper, then a webmaster, then a programmer. I tried being a programmer for a while and went back to school to get qualified to teach.

I did that for a while, then I became a programmer again, and now I'm a writer.

It certainly would have been simpler if I had wanted to be a veterinarian from the time I was three, attended college and vet school, started working as a vet, and stayed in that career until I retired. I admire the people who can do that, but for most of us, it's not reality.

We may not be clear on what we want to begin with, and even if we are, our tastes and circumstances change, and the world changes. For instance, when I was in junior high, I really wanted to be a writer, specifically a novelist. At the time, that was a really impractical career choice. Unless you had a job with a newspaper or got really lucky, almost nobody could make a living as a writer in those days. However, with the internet and ebooks taking off and rendering the gatekeepers and middlemen increasingly obsolete, my dream of making a living as a writer is much more feasible now.

If you can accept some uncertainty and leave your path and your plans flexible, you don't need to fear external change nearly as much as someone with a more rigid approach. For example, many journalists are lamenting the imminent death of the newspaper business as we know it and proclaiming that nobody can make a living as a writer any more! They see the same changes that are empowering me as spelling their doom. But they're far more established than I am and have the benefit of years of name recognition and large audiences. If they embraced the new world, they could use those advantages and do great.

If you start with the expectation that you'll be making course corrections, you'll be much better prepared to stay flexible and grow with the times, whatever changes the outside world hands you or you hand yourself.

Think about...

Which of these internal roadblocks do you recognize in your life?

__ Fear of failure

__ Wanting to make a perfect start

__ Confusion or uncertainty

RELEASING THE BRAKES

*H*ave you ever tried to help someone whose car was stuck, and you pushed and pushed, only to discover that the emergency brake was on? Sometimes our lives are like that, too.

Our life brakes can take many forms. A few common ones are confusion, limiting beliefs, and not embracing our power. When we release these, getting unstuck becomes immeasurably easier.

Confusion

Being stuck and being confused go hand in hand. Often part of being stuck is lacking clarity on what we're trying to do or where we're trying to go. If you don't know where you're trying to end up, it's hard to guess what will get you there or where to start.

You may also be afraid but not sure exactly what you're afraid of. Fear loses a lot of its power when it's defined. As a bonus, if you figure out exactly what you're afraid of, you'll often find that your fears are unfounded.

For example, when I started building my Beyond Fear workshop, I found myself filled with anxiety and dread before my interviews with guest speakers. I knew the people I'd be talking to, and I had chosen them because they were nice and had interesting things to say. Yet, as I contemplated interviewing them, I felt as if they were going to reach through the phone and devour me.

I decided to break it down and figure out exactly what I was afraid of. As it turned out, it mainly boiled down to the fear that I would forget how to talk. I was also afraid I would remember how to talk but say stupid things and sound like a fool.

Once I realized that was my big fear, it was much easier to go on and do the interviews. Even if I did say a lot of stupid things or forget how to talk, at worst, I would be embarrassed in front of five people. I could send them emails apologizing, throw away the recording, and never think about it again. It really wasn't worth worrying about or staying stuck over.

I did the interviews, and I was a little awkward, but not humiliatingly so, and as I did more, I got a lot better at it. However, that still didn't stop me from being terrified before my first group coaching call.

This time, when I broke down my fears, I realized that what I was most afraid of was that I didn't have someone else committed to talking. Whereas before I was afraid of the guest speakers, now I was afraid to go on without them! What if none of the participants talked or asked any questions? What if nobody said a thing and everyone realized how socially inept I was?

Again, I realized that there was really very little to fear. At worst, if nobody had anything to say, I could end the call. If nobody *ever* had anything to say, I could discontinue the calls altogether and use that time for other projects.

As I do things and break down what I'm afraid of, surprisingly often I find that my biggest fear is being laughed at. What if I try this and it doesn't work out? Everyone will know I'm a fool and laugh at me!

Although that may have been true in high school, how many

times has it happened in your adult life? My friends laugh at me in a fond way all the time, but that's different. I can't think of any time in my adult life that I've known about anyone taking pleasure at my expense and laughing at me.

When I see someone fail, I feel bad for them and hope things turn around soon. That's how most people are. We want each other to succeed and be happy.

Even when people do see things go wrong for you, and even if they remember it (which they usually don't), it just makes them all the more impressed later when you do achieve your goal.

But what about more serious fears than being laughed at? After all, fear is there for a reason: to warn us and keep us out of danger.

If you have a fear that may be legitimate, it still helps to define it. You can perform risk analysis to determine whether the outcome you stand to gain is worth the risk. Or, you can do the shorthand version: as you're faced with a decision, think about what you want to remember as you look back on your life, and make the choice that will get you there.

Think about...

What fears are holding you back?

_____

_____

_____

_____

_____

_____

_____

Can you break them down into simpler or more basic root fears?

_____

_____

_____

_____

_____

_____

_____

What are you really afraid of—what do you think might happen?

_____

_____

_____

_____

_____

_____

How likely is the scenario you fear?

_____

_____

_____

_____

_____

What's a more likely outcome?

_____

_____

_____

_____

_____

How have you handled similar situations in the past?

_____

_____

_____

_____

_____

_____

What old, obsolete fears do you still carry from your past?

_____

_____

_____

_____

_____

_____

_____

How can you remind yourself that these old fears are no longer valid or relevant in your life?

_____

_____

_____

_____

List the 10 most recent things you've been afraid of. How many came true?

_____

_____

_____

_____

_____

_____

_____

_____

_____

_____

_____

_____

For the decision you're facing now or the change you're hesitating on, imagine looking back on your life when you are old. Which option would you rather remember taking?

_____

_____

_____

_____

The past and other people

Another form our brakes can take is our circumstances. We look around and see all of the things holding us back and conclude that it's always going to be this way.

What's worse, many of us feel like our relationships or past events are holding us back. *If I hadn't had such a screwed-up childhood, I would be happy now. If my husband didn't spend all my money, I could go to art school. If I had chosen a different major in college, I would be living the life of my dreams now.*

Whether these things are true or not, they don't have to hold you back. You may be starting at a disadvantage, but plenty of people have started there and still achieved great things.

It's time to let go of the past and the option to blame other people. You control your life, and you get to choose how the rest of it is going to be.

It may feel like you have no power and no choices. You may feel completely trapped. It's time to take a closer look at your situation and find out where you're giving away your power.

Your Feelings

Have you ever said (or thought), "he makes me so angry!" or "she makes me miserable!"? If you're like me, only about a million times!

But actually, it's not that simple. It's not the events or people's actions that cause our feelings. Think about how many times you've been in a situation that you found very upsetting, but other people didn't seem to mind. You've probably also experienced the opposite and wondered why the other person was getting so upset.

In reality, our feelings are caused more by our interpretation of events than by the events themselves.[3] For example, if you're riding in a car with a professional race car driver and he does a sharp turn or brakes suddenly, your reaction would probably be very different than if you were riding with your teenage son and he did the same thing.

The difference is in how you see the situation. Because you're more likely to trust the professional driver to know what he's doing and have the situation under control, you're less likely to feel threatened or in danger if he makes a sudden move.

In any situation, the way you feel is determined by what you believe and how you interpret the situation. Knowing this, you can change the way you feel and react to situations. If you've ever wished things didn't upset you so much, here's how to make that a reality.

— **Don't take things personally.** If someone cuts you off in traffic or blocks the aisle in the grocery store, you could get angry and upset about how rude or inconsiderate the person is, or you could let it roll off your back. If you believe people do these things intentionally to insult you, of course you're going to be angry. But if you acknowledge that you really don't know why the other person did that, you can probably think of other, more plausible reasons. Maybe the rude driver is taking his wife to the hospital, and she's in labor right now. Maybe the shopper can't think straight because her mother is ill.

It may seem like people are out to get you, but in most cases, they're just thoughtless.

What's more, most of the time, you'll never know the real reason, so you might as well assume it's nothing to do with you and save yourself a lot of suffering.[4] To save energy, I don't even make up individual stories for each incident. I just assume all rude people are desperate for a bathroom. When you look at things that way, it's much easier to shrug them off and get on with your life.

— **Don't extrapolate.** If something happens and you immediately foresee a chain of further disasters or assume that everything will always be like this one event, you're making yourself miserable for no reason. You don't know what will happen next, so there's no point getting upset about it.

Meanwhile, maybe you can do something to improve your chances that this won't be a disaster. Think about how you could contain the damage. Is there anything you can do to prevent similar things from happening in the future? Is there any way you can turn the situation around and make it a win?

For example, I set up interviews with ten other bloggers for my Beyond Fear workshop. A week and a half before he was scheduled to be interviewed, one of my interviewees sent me a confrontational email saying that he didn't believe I could deliver what I was promising in the workshop, so he was pulling out.

It would have been easy to freak out, be offended and insulted that he was calling my honor into question, and go into a tailspin worrying about whether he would ruin my good name all over the internet. What if all the other interviewees dropped out, too? On top of that, what would the participants think? What if they all wanted their money back and nobody ever bought anything from me again?

But instead, I took a step back. To be honest, imagining that he desperately needed to pee didn't really offer a satisfying explanation for this email. However, the larger picture of the human condition is that we're all screwed up in some way. When we attack each other, it's out of our own pain and inability to handle things gracefully. Although I considered whether there might be merit to what he was saying, I generally dismissed the whole incident as his problem, not mine.

On top of that, I was really glad I didn't have to interview him if that's the way he felt about the workshop! Instead, I contacted the participants to see if they might like a week off. I had been desperately wanting a break, but didn't want to throw the schedule off or reschedule all of the remaining interviewees. His canceling presented a golden opportunity, and it turned out they were as happy as I was to get a break. We shifted that week's content later in the workshop and carried on. I also found a replacement interviewee who ended up being even more inspiring and interesting than the one who backed out.

That's what I mean about turning the situation into a win. Look for the silver lining or how you could turn it around. At the very least, focus on what you can do to contain the damage and be better prepared for the future.

— **Be careful what you tell yourself.** If you react to a situation by thinking over and over about how terrible or awful it is or how you can't stand it, you just upset yourself. That accomplishes nothing and feels horrible. You can acknowledge that you don't like what happened, but don't fall into the trap of ruminating on it and getting yourself all worked up.

When something happens that we don't like, our minds tend to go over it again and again in attempt to make sense of it. The less sense something makes to us, the more we tend to fixate on it. In a way, we can't fault our minds: their job is to try to make sense of things. But many things that happen have no reason, logic, or sense. No matter how many times we go over them, they will never make sense to us because they simply don't make sense.

You can help yourself by giving your mind something else to do. Focus on solutions. Instead of thinking "why why why???" or "how could someone do something like that?" or "this is terrible!", ask yourself, "How can this be all right?"[5] If you find yourself straying back into the freakout realm, just keep redirecting your thoughts back to looking for ways to cope and make it turn out ok. This may be difficult at first, but it gets easier with practice.

Recognizing Your Choices

As you think about your life, you may notice yourself saying things like "I have to..." a lot. "I should," "I have to," and "I can't" go together and embody the way it feels to be stuck. It's not a good feeling! We want so much more out of our lives, but it seems impossible to move at all from where we are now.

In fact, it's not impossible. It's mostly our fear of change and inertia that keep us where we are. "Have to"s and "can't"s reinforce that. They also give us an excuse for staying where we are. After all, we're just doing what we have to—who would fault us for something we can't control?

The reality of our lives as adults in a free society is that we don't have to do anything. Don't want to go to work tomorrow?

Don't want to listen to your kids whine every day? You could slip out the back door tonight, go live in the wilderness, and never come back. Don't like the wilderness? Get a job on a cruise ship instead. Don't like cruises? Move to Thailand and do consulting over the internet. Don't really want to leave home? Stay but pinch your kids whenever they whine. Don't believe in corporal punishment? Instead of pinching them, leave the room.

As you read these absurd suggestions, you may realize that you don't actually want to leave your current life behind, you just want to change a few small things about it. In fact, it may be that you take care of your kids, not because you have to, but because you love them, and you really wouldn't want to be away from them. It may be that you go to work, not because you have to, but because you know how to do it and you need the income. It may be that you stay in your town, not because you have to, but because you have friends, you know where everything is, and you don't want to go to the trouble of moving.

In reality, there are thousands of choices out there. We don't want to do most of them, but just knowing they're out there can relieve the feeling of being trapped. Knowing that we choose to do what we do for our own reasons is powerful. You really do have the power to control and shape your own life if you choose to use it.

As you realize you do have choices, you can change your thinking. Instead of "I can't..." start thinking "How can I...?" What other choices do you have, and how could you change what you're doing to get closer to what you want?

As you think of the other choices available, you may find that your current situation actually looks pretty good. That's a valuable mental shift, but be careful not to use "this isn't so bad—it could be a lot worse" as an excuse to stay in a situation that's not really meeting your needs. It's important to see the good in our lives, and it's empowering to recognize that we do everything we do by choice. Once you acknowledge that, use it to see your situation clearly, separate what you want from what you don't want, and start getting more of what you want.

For example, when I was in debt and hated my job, I caught myself thinking "I have to go to work and do all this boring crap that suuuuuuucks!" But really, I didn't have to go to work. I could just stop showing up and never go back there again.

It's so far outside the realm of what normal people do, it almost sounds impossible, but it's true. Nobody was going to come to my house and drag me in to the office or beat me or take me to prison if I didn't go. The world wouldn't end. Time wouldn't stop.

However, I would almost certainly get fired. Since I needed the money and wanted a good recommendation in the event that I applied for another job, suddenly going to work seemed like it was in my best interest. So I went.

I also thought about how I could get my need (for money, in this case) met some other way so I could eventually ditch the job. I aggressively paid off debts and socked away a freedom fund, and I started a business on the side. In July, I turned in my notice and really did stop showing up for work, just like I wanted.

It's important to realize that your change may not be the kind that can happen all at once. If it was easy, you probably wouldn't be stuck. But claiming your power is the first step. If you realize you have choices and start looking at why you do what you do, and what else you could be doing instead, suddenly you're a whole lot less trapped.

From now on, whenever you do something, own it. Realize that you are choosing to do it, and why. If you don't want to do something and can't think of a good reason to do it, then don't do it. By doing this, you place yourself in control of your life. That makes it a whole lot easier to get unstuck.

Stop Making Excuses

The companion of "I have to..." is "I can't..." Like "I have to...", "I can't..." represents giving up our power.

Of course, there are some things we truly can't do. For instance, as much as I'd like to, I can't fly more than three feet without mechanical assistance. But many times, when we tell ourselves we can't, we're just making excuses. I used to do this a lot: I can't concentrate, I can't code, I can't read, I can't write, I can't function in the morning, I think I have ADD. The sad thing is, when I was confronted with work I didn't want to do, I really believed these things.

It was only when I caught myself in counterexamples that I realized I was just giving myself excuses. One time, soon after I had started my blog, I was putting off editing a user guide at work. After accomplishing nothing on it for almost two weeks, I caught myself thinking "I just can't do this word stuff." Meanwhile, in my free time, I was writing all these blog posts, reading books about how to become a better writer, and blabbing about how much I love writing and want to be a writer!

Once I called myself on my bogus excuse, I settled down to work and did a great job on the user guide. In fact, approaching it from the perspective of being good at this sort of thing, I thought of a whole new section that should be in there and added it, making the guide much more meaningful and helpful for the users.

Since then, I've been on the lookout for my bogus excuses. Each time I catch myself saying "can't," I look harder to see if it's really true. Most of the time, it's not.

I encourage you to do this for your life, too. Instead of automatically thinking "I can't do that," don't let that be the final answer. If you really can't do it now, what would it take for you to be able to? Do you need a different working environment, more information, skills, help? Ask yourself, "How could I do this if I really needed to?" If it's something important to you, pursue that.

If it turns out you actually don't *want* to do whatever it is, that's ok—just realize that's why you're not doing it. When you think you can't, you're stuck. When you choose not to do something, you have control of your life.

Think about...

Do you feel like events from your past are holding you back now? If so, what happened?

_____

_____

_____

_____

_____

_____

_____

_____

_____

Do you feel like other people are holding you back? If so, who?

_____

_____

_____

_____

_____

_____

_____

_____

What small steps could you take to shift your life more toward what you want it to be?

_____

_____

_____

_____

_____

How could you override the influence of the past or people?

_____

_____

_____

_____

_____

_____

Do you find yourself getting upset in situations where others are not upset?

_____

_____

What causes the difference between their reaction and yours?

_____

_____

_____

Are you:

__ taking things personally

__ extrapolating from the situation to predict disaster

__ telling yourself upsetting things about the situation

How would your life be different if you reacted calmly to unpleasant situations?

_____

_____

_____

_____

_____

_____

_____

_____

If you adopted a less upsettable approach to life, what would you gain? What would you lose?

_____

_____

_____

_____

_____

_____

_____

Observe your thought patterns and what you say. Which of these do you use a lot?

___ have to

___ should

___ can't

Do these phrases represent your life accurately?

_____

_____

_____

When you think about the situations you normally describe with these phrases, what other options do you have? Brainstorm at least five, even if they're silly or impractical.

_____

_____

_____

_____

_____

_____

_____

_____

_____

_____

How could you change what you're doing to get closer to what you want?

_____

_____

_____

_____

_____

_____

What would it take for you to be able to do what you "can't" or not do what you "have to"? How could you make it happen if you really needed to?"

_____

_____

_____

_____

_____

_____

_____

_____

_____

_____

Limiting beliefs and faulty assumptions

Limiting beliefs are another form of brakes: they're beliefs that hold us back. Some examples include I'm not good enough, everything worth doing is a struggle, only lucky people are successful, or life is a vale of tears.

You may not realize you have these beliefs. One particularly insidious one is the belief that money is evil, or rich people are bad. A lot of people with Christian backgrounds are particularly prone to these beliefs. First of all, the Bible says "the love of money is the root of all evil," not money itself. Money is not evil. It's just a tool, and it can be used for great good. It seems absurd to try to be a virtuous person by making foolish choices and continually going into debt, but many people do just that, while looking with derision on anyone with a savings account as someone who doesn't trust the Lord to provide.

Another prime area for limiting beliefs is success. We often fear success for a variety of reasons. If I do well at this, people will expect more of me from now on. If I succeed, people I care about may be envious and not want to be around me any more. Some of this may be carryover from school, when doing well meant being called a curve-wrecker and a nerd. You may also be afraid that if you do well, it takes away from others' chance of success.

In reality, most people are happy to see others succeed. The people who like you want you to be happy. What's more, there is plenty of success to go around. You may find a few people who are put off if you succeed, but that's a sign of an unhealthy relationship. Those who have your best interests at heart will be happy for you.

There are many more limiting beliefs. Some are close to the surface; when they get deeper, we often identify them with ourselves. Instead of "It's bad to be selfish," a deeper belief might be "I'm selfish." Deeper yet: "I'm a selfish, bad person."

These beliefs can also take the form of "I'm not ___ enough," (smart, good, tall, cute, agile, rich, whatever), "I'm too___," (old, fat, ugly, stupid, lazy, etc.), or "I'm ___" (unlucky, sickly, clumsy, unlovable, cursed).

In short, many of our limiting beliefs say, "I'm not good enough."

Common patterns of faulty thinking

You probably have a lot of limiting beliefs yourself, and the first step is to stop identifying with them and reinforcing them. False and unhelpful thoughts fall into a number of common patterns. If you know the patterns, it's easier to recognize the false thoughts and dispute them. Here are a few:

— **All or nothing thinking.** You see everything in black and white. Either you're the best or you're a loser. Your project is perfect or you feel like a failure. You can't see the middle ground: almost everything has some bad and some good.

— **Overgeneralization.** You extrapolate from one or two incidents and assume they represent the entire universe. For example, if one person snubs you, you conclude that nobody likes you. If someone cuts you off in traffic on your way to work, you assume the whole day is going to suck. If one bad thing happens, you conclude that you're unlucky.

The problem with this one is, once you come to this conclusion, you'll be on the lookout for evidence to support it, and our expectations determine how we experience things. Just like when you learn a new word and suddenly hear it everywhere, if you're looking for bad luck and expecting it to happen, you'll see it everywhere. You could go through the same day expecting good luck, and that's what you'd notice instead.

— **Disqualifying the positive.** Here, you filter your experiences to back up your negative conclusions. For example, if you think you're a loser, then any time you do something well or others compliment you, you dismiss it as a fluke or come up with a reason why it doesn't count. But any time you do something badly or someone rejects you, you cling to it as further evidence you were right all along.

— **Jumping to conclusions.** Based on one incident, you assume you know what others are thinking and what will happen next. For instance, if someone doesn't call you, you assume it's because he doesn't like you any more. If you feel bad, you assume you'll be alone and miserable for the rest of your life.

— **Blowing things out of proportion.** When you make a mistake or something goes wrong, you make a huge deal about it and think it's terrible, horrible, and awful. But when you do something right, you think it's inconsequential and not worth mentioning.

— **Emotional reasoning.** You assume that if you feel a certain way, it means you are that way. For example, if you feel sad, you assume you must have a tragic life. If you feel guilty, you must have done something wrong. If you feel angry, someone must have wronged you.

— **The shoulds.** You believe you should do this and you must do that. If you don't, you feel inadequate. You also believe others should and shouldn't do things, according to your set of beliefs about how the world should work. Any time you think a "should," you're focusing on what's not instead of life as it really is. It's much more productive to face reality head on.[6]

Watch for thoughts that follow these patterns and dispute them whenever you encounter them.

We tend to filter our experiences by what we already believe: we generally notice things that match our beliefs and miss things that contradict them. So if you believe you're incompetent, there's a good chance you'll notice all of the small things that go wrong and use them to reinforce the belief that you can't do anything right.

If you discourage yourself enough to give up trying, your belief becomes a self-fulfilling prophecy. To break that cycle, you have to stop identifying with the belief. You will still encounter things that seem to "prove" the belief was true, but it's time to look at them differently. When something goes wrong, try to look at it as an isolated incident rather than further proof that you can't do anything right.

As you observe yourself and catch yourself in these patterns or other unhelpful thoughts, remember to be compassionate with yourself. Everyone uses faulty thinking sometimes, and it takes practice to change your habits and think differently. When you catch yourself, don't beat yourself up; just patiently substitute a more helpful thought instead.

Faulty Assumptions

We all use our experiences to build mental maps of how the world works. Then we use our mental maps to guide us in our interactions with people and the world. For instance, most people learn at a young age that hot things hurt, so it's smart to avoid touching them. We build our maps by trial and error or by listening to others' advice—either way, we record the information so we can avoid the same problem in the future.

The benefits are obvious: if we had to keep learning not to

touch hot stuff over and over, we'd burn ourselves every time we tried to make dinner.

The problem comes in when the information in our maps is wrong. Maybe we generalized from a situation that isn't as general as we thought, maybe we misinterpreted what happened, or maybe others gave us inaccurate information.

Imagine if the first time you ever met a dog, it snarled and attacked you. You would probably conclude that dogs are dangerous and should be avoided whenever possible. That is true in your experience, but not in the general case. Most dogs are nice, but you'll never discover that if your mental map tells you to avoid dogs.

When we act based on inaccurate mental maps, it causes trouble. What's worse, we usually don't know what went wrong, so it's hard to correct. The assumptions in our mental maps are so long-held, we're usually not even aware of them as anything but truth. That's why we keep acting on them and causing ourselves the same problems over and over.

Many of the contents of our mental maps are written during childhood and interactions with our families. As we observe how our families work, we assume that's how the world works. Here are a few examples I picked up during my childhood:

— The worst thing you can be is selfish.

— If I have to ask for something, it doesn't count as a gift, even if the other person gives it to me.

— Never complain—nobody likes people who complain.

— There's one right way to do things, and they better be done that way.

Operating with faulty assumptions in your mental map is a recipe for disaster, like going on a road trip with an inaccurate road map. But if you don't know what your assumptions are or what's wrong with them, how can you find out and do better?

One good place to start is by looking at what has gone wrong, tracing that back to what you did and how you acted, and then exploring why you acted that way. You may be able to unearth the faulty assumptions at the root of many of your problems. It's often hard to see those things by yourself. Sometimes it takes an outside perspective to be able to spot the faulty assumptions. You may need to talk to a friend, coach, or therapist, and have him or her help you find the holes and misinformation.

There are a few common ones that I can point out here, though. This list is from *How to Keep People from Pushing Your Buttons,* and it includes many of the common faulty assumptions that keep us stuck.[7]

Other people's opinion of you is crucial, and if they reject you, it means you're worthless.

This one keeps you stuck by making it scary to try anything unexpected. But by staying safe, you limit yourself to the lowest common denominator, the bland baby food version of yourself. You keep yourself from being fully you, doing what you want, and realizing your dreams.

If something goes wrong, it's somebody's fault. You better make sure it's not yours.

Trying to avoid being blamed is another great way to get stuck. It's hard to do anything interesting while keeping your head down.

Worrying about something will make it turn out better than if you didn't worry.

If you can turn your worry into action, it can help you. For example, if your worry causes you to buy a fire extinguisher or take a precaution for a legitimate risk, that's useful. However, must of us don't do it that way. We just sit around and stew over what might happen. That's a waste of energy.

Here's one of my favorite stories about worry. A. J. Jacobs, editor-at-large at Esquire magazine, did a life experiment where he outsourced his responsibilities to personal assistants in India. First he had his assistants doing research and clerical tasks, then he had them take over his correspondence. He kept giving them more assignments as he thought of things he didn't like doing.

Finally, he realized he was spending a lot of energy worrying about a big project he was working on, and decided to try outsourcing his worry. He didn't outsource the project, just worrying about it. He asked his assistant, Honey, if she would worry about it in his stead. She promised: "I will worry about this every day. Do not worry." It worked: "Every time I started to ruminate, I'd remind myself that Honey was already on the case, and I'd relax."[8]

After I read this, I realized I was worrying about a lot of things, and it wasn't accomplishing anything. I don't have an assistant in India, but A. J. does, and I figured if she's already worrying about his stuff, it's not much more trouble to worry about mine, too. So I decided to pretend to outsource my worrying to her. Every time I felt myself beginning to worry or dwell on something upsetting, I just told myself Honey was on that and I could stop.

Nothing came out any worse for my not angsting over it, and I felt a whole lot better. Over time, short-circuiting my worrying this way has become a habit, and I worry much less.

It is easier to avoid difficult situations and responsibilities than to face them.

It's true that in the short term, it feels better to avoid your problems and work. That's one way we get stuck.

The longer you avoid dealing with something, the more you dread it, the worse it feels, and the more you want to keep avoiding it. Most problems don't go away on their own. It's better to deal with them and get them out of the way.

> *You can protect yourself from getting hurt by never caring too deeply or investing yourself too much in any pursuit.*

Staying safely detached is another form of staying stuck. We're afraid of being hurt, being wrong, or looking foolish, so we don't take risks, and we try not to care what happens.

It doesn't work, though. We still get hurt. By trying to play it safe, we keep from giving our all to projects or relationships. That often leads to failure in the long run. Ironically, we cause the very thing we were trying to protect ourselves against.

> *Bad people and things shouldn't exist, so if they do, you have to get upset about them.*

Another way to stay stuck is to waste energy worrying about what other people do or what happens outside your control. The world is what it is; you can get upset if you want to, but it doesn't help anything, and it feels terrible. It's far better to focus on the things you can control (i.e., yourself and what you do) and act.

Perfectionism

Perfectionism causes so much stuckness, it could fill its own book. At its heart, perfectionism is the fear of not being good enough. Many of us have the idea that if we screw up or fail, nobody will love us and everybody will laugh at us. So we try to do everything perfectly to keep those things from happening.

If you suffer from this belief, consider this: are your friends perfect? When they make a mistake, do you hate them and scorn them? That would be ridiculous—they're only human, right?

Everybody makes mistakes. *That includes you.* In fact, nothing gets discovered or created without any mistakes. How many times did Thomas Edison try to invent the light bulb before he actually came up with something that worked?

I suggest abandoning the notion of failure altogether. No matter what you do, you're going to make mistakes. If you learn from them, those mistakes will form part of your valuable knowledge and experience. They'll give you what you need to achieve your later goals. In fact, some of the worst disasters of my life have provided the most valuable foundation for my current success.

Remember, the scientist who invented Post-It Notes was trying to create a super permanent adhesive when he developed the formula for the removable, restickable adhesive that makes Post-It Notes possible. He utterly failed at what he was trying to do, but he created a success worth millions.[9]

Impostor Syndrome

When you take perfectionism and limiting beliefs to an extreme, one possible outcome is impostor syndrome. People who suffer from impostor syndrome are generally successful people with lots of achievements, but they don't believe they're really as smart or competent as everyone thinks. What's worse, they're afraid it's only a matter of time before everyone discovers the truth about them.

If you have impostor syndrome, no matter how successful you are or what you achieve, you don't believe you've really earned your successes with your talents and abilities. You always write it off as luck, knowing the right people, being charming, or being in the right place at the right time.[10]

For example, when people used to try to praise me for my grades in college, I always evaded the praise by saying that I was just good at playing the system—I could sniff out what teachers wanted to hear and easily feed it back to them, and I was good at test-taking.

Because we don't really believe we've earned our successes, any time self-styled impostors are called on to do something similar or meet a new challenge, we're afraid we'll fail and everyone will finally see how incompetent we really are.

If you think this might be you, here are a few common characteristics. People with impostor syndrome:

— are filled with self-doubt and worry.

— remember obstacles, failures, and negative feedback more readily than their successes.

— think much more about what they don't know than what they do.

— feel inadequate if they're not the best at what they do.

— place unreasonable demands on themselves, expecting themselves to do everything perfectly.

— have a strong fear of failure and go to extreme lengths to make sure they never fail at anything.

— discount praise and deny their own competence.

— experience guilt and fear of success.

Impostor syndrome can paralyze you and keep you stuck, so it's important to step outside yourself and take a more objective look at what's happening. Impostor syndrome is a distortion of reality; you can release yourself by replacing it with a more accurate view.

As you approach something you're afraid you'll fail at, ask yourself: have I succeeded at similar things in the past? How many times have I truly failed? Is it really likely that I'll fail at this? If I did, what's the worst that would happen?

Also, when friends or colleagues praise or congratulate you, instead of disagreeing or jumping in with an excuse, take a step back and consider. Could this person be right?

It takes time to change deep-seated views of yourself like im-postor syndrome, but you can. Accepting praise and owning your accomplishments doesn't have to make you stuck-up or arrogant. All you have to do is smile and say "thank you." That's far more gracious and pleasant for those around you than discounting praise or arguing with compliments.

Most importantly, stop being so hard on yourself. Allow your-self to try things you might not succeed at, and give yourself credit when you do things well. A more realistic, well-rounded view of life will serve you well and make you less likely to get stuck.

Think about...

Which of these patterns of faulty thinking do you find yourself using?

__ All or nothing thinking

__ Overgeneralization

__ Disqualifying the positive

__ Jumping to conclusions

__ Blowing things out of proportion

__ Emotional reasoning

__ The shoulds

When you think in these ways, does it make you feel better, or worse?

_____

_____

_____

_____

_____

_____

Are the thoughts generated by these patterns accurate?

_____

_____

_____

_____

What happens as a result of your thinking this way? How does it impact yourself and/or the world around you?

_____

_____

_____

_____

_____

_____

_____

Which of these limiting beliefs and faulty assumptions do you recognize from your life?

__ Money is evil

__ Everyone hates successful people

__ I'm not _____ enough to get what I want

__ I'm too _____ to do what I want

__ My life is a mess because I'm _____

__ The worst thing you can be is selfish.

__ If I have to ask for something, it doesn't count as a gift, even if the other person gives it to me.

__ Never complain—nobody likes people who complain.

__ There's one right way to do things, and they better be done that way.

__ Other people's opinion of you is crucial, and if they reject you, it means you're worthless.

__ If something goes wrong, it's somebody's fault. You better make sure it's not yours.

__ Worrying about something will make it turn out better than if you didn't worry.

__ It is easier to avoid difficult situations and responsibilities than to face them.

__ You can protect yourself from getting hurt by never caring too deeply or investing yourself too much in any pursuit.

__ Bad people and things shouldn't exist, so if they do, you have to get upset about them.

__ I must be perfect or I will be rejected.

For each belief you recognize, how could you dispute it? Can you think of a counter-example?

_____

_____

_____

_____

_____

_____

_____

_____

_____

_____

_____

_____

When you think of a time when your life didn't go as planned, can you trace your actions back to any faulty assumptions?

_____

_____

_____

_____

_____

_____

_____

What would your friends add to this list for you?

_____

_____

_____

_____

Do you believe imperfect people are worthy of love? Why or why not?

_____

_____

_____

_____

_____

Can you love yourself, even when you make mistakes?

_____

_____

Do you believe you're less smart or competent than others think?

_____

_____

_____

What truths about yourself do you fear others discovering?

_____

_____

_____

_____

_____

_____

_____

_____

Do you have a hard time accepting compliments or praise? If so, why do you think that is?

_____

_____

_____

_____

_____

List some of the times you've succeeded or achieved your
goals in the past.

_____

_____

_____

_____

_____

_____

_____

_____

_____

If the list belonged to someone other than yourself, would you
be impressed?

_____

_____

_____

_____

_____

_____

_____

_____

_____

More Tools

Depending what form your stuckness takes, you may find different shifts of thought or outlook helpful. Here are the ones that have helped me the most.

Brain Dump

Sometimes I find myself feeling really anxious and flailing around a lot, jumping from task to task afraid I'll miss something, and unable to focus on anything or even complete a thought. I can't decide what to do first because there's so much to do, it all seems crucial, and I can't even hold it all in my head at the same time to make a proper comparison.

It helps to understand what's going on in times like these. When you try to decide what to do next or try not to forget something, you're using your prefrontal cortex. The prefrontal cortex is responsible for activities like recalling, deciding, understanding, memorizing, prioritizing, and pushing aside distractions. It uses a ton of energy and isn't very powerful compared to the rest of your brain. To get an idea of scale, the prefrontal cortex is to the rest of your brain as the coins in your pocket are to the entire US economy prior to the crash of 2008.[11]

Trying not to forget something is very taxing, and the pre-frontal cortex can only do one thing at a time. If you're trying to remember things and also trying to make a decision, you're attempting something your brain is not built to do.

Instead, make a list. Better yet, represent things visually—that brings in other, more powerful areas of your brain to help.[12]

It's amazing how much tension you can release just by writing things down instead of storing them in your head and trying not to let any of them slip away. When I find myself getting into an anxious flail, I take ten minutes to write down everything I need to do, big or small, important or not. Once I have the list, I can go through it and pick out the few most important or most urgent things and start with them. (It also helps to realize that many urgent tasks are not necessarily important.)

Meanwhile, I know all of the other things will be there on the piece of paper when I get back. That lets me release them from my mind and stop wasting energy trying not to forget them.

If you have deeper worries or concerns than to-do items, I recommend doing a freewrite for half an hour. Don't think too much or try to produce quality prose. Don't edit at all. Just spew your thoughts onto paper. This technique helps me get clear on what's bothering me, which makes it much easier to figure out what to do about it. If you don't like writing, you might try painting or music instead; writing is what works for me.

Think about...

What are you trying to hold in your head right now? Do a quick brain dump and get it out.

_____

_____

_____

_____

_____

_____

_____

_____

_____

_____

_____

_____

_____

_____

_____

_____

_____

_____

_____

_____

To-quit list

Sometimes stuckness comes from dread and too many things to do.

I used to feel this way every morning: look at the day, groan, and wish I could go back to bed.

I call it my dread cloud. Gotta do the bills, don't know if I have enough money to pay them all, should have done it days ago... Gotta call people back who are probably mad that I haven't already called them back... Gotta do job stuff that I'm not really sure how to do and has already taken way longer than expected and everybody probably thinks I'm a big slacker...

Sometimes a to-do list is your friend, especially if the tasks are small and not too arduous. But if your to-do list is full of tasks that are intimidating or unpleasant, looking at it is a great way to get more depressed.

What if you started a to-quit list? Instead of trying to do everything on your to-do list, what if you went through it and crossed off everything you didn't want to do?[13]

If your reflex reaction is "I can't do that!", I totally understand, because that's what I thought when I first heard the idea. The idea of quitting everything I didn't like was so foreign and drastic, I was almost afraid to even think about it. But the idea was so tantalizing, in the end, I couldn't resist it.

You don't have to be afraid of thinking about what you want to quit or what you'd like your life to be. You won't derail your life just by thinking. You can think anything you want; you still have control over whether you act on it or not.

When you think of all the things you wish you could quit, but you can't, remember that "can't" is usually an oversimplification. At the time when I read about the idea of the to-quit list, if I was honest with myself, most of my life at the time belonged on the to-quit list. I would have quit it all if I thought I could. In my case, "I can't do that!" meant, "I can't accept the consequences of quitting everything right away, so I choose not to. But I can quit these eight things and look for opportunities to quit more in the future."

I started with small things that didn't really matter: clubs I didn't like going to, volunteer work I did only out of guilt, household tasks that really didn't need doing or could be done by someone else.

I had agreed to sit on the board of directors for my church and serve as treasurer, but there was no way I had time to do that with a full-time job, starting a business on the side, moving, and a marriage on the rocks. I was already dropping half the balls I was trying to juggle; picking up a big one like that was a no-go. I felt horrible about it, but I backed out. It ended up being better for me and for them: they found someone else who did a much better job than I would have in my harried state.

Over time, I've even quit the huge things: my long commute, my expensive house, my disastrous marriage, and finally, my job. As a result, my life feels completely different now. I got unstuck, and I'm a thousand times happier.

For each of your hated tasks, I recommend asking yourself some questions:

— Why is it on the list?

— What do you hate about it? Is there a way to accomplish the same thing without being so miserable?

— What would happen if you just didn't do it? Could you handle the consequences?

— If not, how could you get out of it? Can you delegate it to someone else? rearrange your life so it no longer needs to be done? get the same benefits another way?

— Or would it be simpler to just finish the dang thing already and check it off? If so, do that. Start today.

As you look at your list, pick the most-hated thing on it and imagine how you'd feel if it was gone. Now imagine giving the axe to the whole top five and waking up without them hanging over your head. What a rush!

I'm not advising you to be hasty or ignore the consequences. Just open your mind to what is possible in the long term. You probably can quit most or all of the things on your list over time if you decide to. Even things you don't hate but don't really enjoy are candidates. When you have less to do, you have less to keep up with, less to dread, and more time for the things that are most important to you.

Think about...

As you think over your to-do list, what do you want to move to your to-quit list?

_____

_____

_____

_____

_____

_____

_____

_____

_____

_____

How would it feel to quit all of those things?

_____

_____

_____

_____

_____

What will you quit immediately?

_____

_____

_____

_____

_____

What can you do to get closer to quitting the others?

_____

_____

_____

_____

For each item on the list,

Why is it on the list?

_____

_____

_____

_____

_____

_____

What do you hate about it? Is there a way to accomplish the same thing without being so miserable?

_____

_____

_____

_____

_____

_____

_____

_____

What would happen if you just didn't do it? Could you handle the consequences?

_____

_____

_____

_____

_____

_____

_____

_____

If not, how could you get out of it? Can you delegate it to someone else? Rearrange your life so it no longer needs to be done? get the same benefits another way?

Or would it be simpler just to do it? If so, when will you do it?

Filtering your thoughts

One of the best things I ever learned about being happier is "don't believe everything you think."[14] We all know that our eyes and ears can deceive us, our hearts don't always have the best judgment, and our hormones can lead us astray. My thoughts were the one thing I thought I could rely on. But as we saw in the earlier sections on faulty thinking and assumptions, many of our thoughts are distorted or inaccurate.

You don't have to let these thoughts live in your head and keep holding you back. When you find yourself thinking anything that doesn't feel good, question it. Is it really true? Do I know for certain? Can I think of a counterexample? Is there another way I could look at this that's also true but less painful?

Some of our unpleasant thoughts are true, unfortunately. But many of them are based on pure speculation. There's no need to let those thoughts hang around. By disputing your false thoughts and looking for ways to reframe situations, you can save yourself a lot of needless suffering.

Think about...

Have you ever noticed thinking about something and feeling better or worse the more you thought about it?

_____

_____

_____

_____

_____

If you could control your feelings by filtering your thoughts, what would that mean for you?

_____

_____

_____

_____

_____

_____

_____

_____

_____

_____

_____

What are some of the thoughts you've had recently that have made you feel worse?

_____

_____

_____

_____

_____

_____

_____

_____

_____

For each one,

    Do you know for sure it's 100% true? Do you have proof?

_____

_____

_____

_____

_____

_____

_____

_____

_____

Are there any counterexamples?

_____

_____

_____

_____

_____

_____

_____

_____

_____

What's another way you could look at the situation that would be less painful?

_____

_____

_____

_____

_____

_____

Being gentle with yourself

Have you ever said "I'm my own worst enemy"? Many of us are. Not only do we get ourselves into messy situations, we beat ourselves up for it once we get there. Our harshness with ourselves enforces our fears, which helps keep us stuck. Often, we don't even realize how much we're hindering ourselves.

For me, beating myself up tied in with my perfectionism. I was critical and harsh in attempt to urge myself on to do better. Also, I thought if I found all of my flaws first, it would hurt less if someone else discovered them. Instead, I just felt bad about myself and was afraid to take risks or try new things.

If you treat yourself this way, it's probably because you're trying to make yourself succeed. You're afraid if you take it easy on yourself, you'll be lazy and won't do anything at all.

But does it work? If your child or best friend was struggling, would you try to help him or her this way?

In fact, studies have shown that when we accept ourselves and treat ourselves with compassion, we exercise more self-discipline, not less. In one experiment, subjects were told they were participating in an experiment about television and food. They were asked to eat a donut while watching a documentary. Then, the television was turned off. The experimental group was reassured that it's normal to eat unhealthy food sometimes, so they didn't need to feel bad about eating the donut. The control group was not given this message.

Next, the subjects were asked to taste-test candy. Each was given three large bowls of different kinds of candy. They were told to try at least one piece of each, but they could eat as much as they liked. Conventional wisdom would expect the reassured folks to lack discipline and eat more. Instead, the experimental group was moderate, while the control group ate more candy and reported more guilt about eating.[15]

I've found this to be true in my own life as well. Since I stopped being so hard on myself and expecting myself to be perfect all the time, I'm much more willing to try things, and I get a lot more done. I really hate being yelled at and will do almost anything to avoid it; knowing that I don't have to worry about getting yelled at in my own head has made me much more willing to take control of my life and risk trying new things. It's made me less afraid of everything.

How can you do this for yourself? Be gentle with yourself. Listen to what you say to yourself, and check it: Is it true? Is it kind? Is it helpful?

If someone said what you were saying to a close friend of yours, would you jump to defend your friend? What would you say? If you wouldn't let someone bully your friends, why would you stand by and let yourself bully yourself?

For example, the first time I tried this, I had just had a fight with a longtime friend who was very good at pushing my buttons. He said some things that upset me, and even though I ended the conversation gracefully, I was still miserable.

None of my other friends or family understood why I still talked to this guy; maybe they were right. *Why hadn't I listened to them? How stupid could I be? What was wrong with me?*

I often said such things to myself, but this time I stopped. Did what I was thinking make sense? Did the fact that I was still talking to someone who had meant a lot to me over the years really imply something was wrong with me? How did his hurtful behavior mean I was stupid?

If one of my other friends heard someone berating me this way, they'd probably say the worst I did was act a little naïve. I might be too nice or too trusting, but I wasn't stupid. In fact, I was going through a pretty difficult time and doing the best I could, so I really didn't need or deserve such harsh judgment. Back off, critical judge.

After having this little talk with myself, I felt amazingly better.

It was like a cloud lifted. What the other person said still hurt, but I no longer felt devastated, humiliated, or miserable; more like "what a pity things turned so ugly."

For years I had been my own worst enemy, and my harshest critic and judge. That night, I started being my own best friend instead.

It takes a little practice, but it's not that hard, and it really works. Any time you feel upset, listen to what you're saying to yourself. If you're thinking about how terrible everything is or beating yourself up, recognize it as faulty thinking and dispute it. Examine each thought. Is it true? Do you have proof? How does it make you feel? Is there another interpretation for the situation that's equally true but not upsetting?

In my case, it's often one copy of my voice in my head (Critical Me) attacking another copy (Weak Me): "You never do anything right. Why are you even trying? You'll fail at this, just like you've failed at tons of other things, and everyone will know! You'll be a laughing stock!"

I've found the quickest way to defuse that is to have a third copy of my voice (Advocate Me) stand up to Critical Me, just like I would stand up to someone who was bullying my friend: "Hey, [me] has done plenty of things right! You can't expect to do things perfectly on the first try, but failing is good—it's part of learning, and it's not permanent unless you quit. Maybe there are some mean people who would laugh if this ends poorly, but probably not, and who cares about them even if they do exist? [Me] is an all right sort who's doing the best she can, so lay off."

The first time I was advised to do this, I have to admit it sounded a little crazy. It's bad enough that I talk to myself; now I'm supposed to argue with myself, too?

But I tried it, and it really helped me. I figure, if I'm already talking to myself anyway, I might as well add another persona—at least that puts the nice ones in the majority!

I don't know why it works, but my guess is that by arguing with my internal critic, I've distanced myself from the harsh judgments. It doesn't feel like they come from me any more. In fact, they hardly come up at all any more. Apparently I've retrained myself to be more accurate and compassionate in my thinking.

That makes a surprising difference. Now it feels like I'll love myself no matter what, whereas before it didn't. And when you really know that you love yourself and always will, it gives you strength. It loosens fear's hold, and other people's opinions matter a lot less. You have a strong foundation within yourself, and it supports you to go out and do bigger and better things.

Think about...

Do you identify with the statement "I'm my own worst enemy?"

_____

_____

_____

How have you been detrimental to your own success in the past?

_____

_____

_____

_____

_____

_____

Do you beat yourself up over your shortcomings? If so, why?

_____

_____

_____

_____

_____

_____

_____

How would your life be different if you treated yourself gently instead?

_____

_____

_____

_____

_____

Think of something your critical voice would say about you right now. What does it sound like?

Is it loud or soft?

_____

Is it a male voice, or female?

_____

Whose voice is it?

_____

How do you feel when you listen to it?

_____

_____

_____

What happens if you try to turn the volume down on it, or replace the voice with Mickey Mouse's voice?

_____

_____

_____

_____

Now consider how you talk to yourself when you're practicing compassion.

What would your nurturing or advocate voice say about you right now?

_____

_____

_____

_____

How does this voice sound—loud, soft, male, female?

_____

_____

Whose voice is it?

_____

_____

How do you feel when you listen to it?

_____

_____

_____

_____

What is your critical voice trying to protect you from or help you do?

_____

_____

_____

_____

_____

_____

_____

Could your nurturing or advocate voice accomplish the same thing?

_____

_____

How would your life be different if you were your own best friend?

_____

_____

_____

_____

_____

_____

_____

Embracing growth

A lot of people think intelligence, or innate talent, is responsible for success. It seems to make sense, but actually, it's not quite true. It's the people who keep growing who come up with the best ideas and are willing to take the risk of trying something new.

When it comes to learning, most people have one of two mindsets: a fixed mindset, or a growth mindset. A fixed mindset assumes your outcomes are determined by your intelligence and talent, which can't be changed. A growth mindset assumes you can get stronger, better, and smarter over time by learning.

A fixed mindset is a subtle trap: If you believe it's your intelligence and talent that determine whether you succeed or fail, things that you don't know seem a lot more threatening because they demonstrate that you don't already have everything you need for success within you.

If you believe that you're smart and people expect it of you, you can become afraid to try new things and appear incompetent. Meanwhile, if you believe that you're dumb, you can also become afraid to try new things, because you believe you're doomed to failure. Both of these responses are symptoms of a fixed mindset, and either way, they stop you from learning and growing. If you don't realize what you're doing, you can build yourself an ever-shrinking comfort zone of stuckness.

If you have a fixed mindset, you probably feel threatened by:

— challenges—what if I don't have what it takes to meet this challenge?

— obstacles—what if I can't figure out how to get around this obstacle?

— having to expend a lot of effort— if talent is what counts, why should I have to work this hard? Will it buy me anything?

- criticism—the things I've done reflect my abilities, so criticism of my work is a criticism of me

- others' success—if they do something I haven't, it's probably because they're smarter or better than me, so I can never catch up, and it makes me look stupid by comparison

- new ideas or approaches—if what I already know isn't enough, that means I'm obsolete

The danger of being a genius or an expert in a certain field is that it's easy to fall into an ego-driven fixed mindset, where you're so busy maintaining your image as the smartest or best, you become afraid to try new things for fear of making a mistake in front of someone. "Experts" often end up very attached to their pet ways of doing things, to the point that they'll fight passionately for their use over other methods, even when their approach really doesn't make sense.

It's not just experts, though. Anyone can fall into the fixed mindset trap. I recognize more of myself in this than I like to admit. Every time I've tried a new hobby, I've found myself frustrated that I wasn't immediately good at it. Roller hockey, spinning yarn, contra dancing, autocross, painting—with each one, I got very frustrated and discouraged at how bad I was at it and how much better everyone else was, even though I knew that was ridiculous. Nobody is born knowing how to do any of those things. Some people pick them up faster than others, but everybody has to learn and practice if they want to get good. That's just how life works. But somehow I still find myself thinking "I'm smart, so I should be good at this!"

The problem with a fixed mindset is that it limits you to never being much better than you are now. In contrast, a growth mindset approaches the brain like a muscle that can be strengthened and developed. Challenges and obstacles are just opportunities to get stronger. Situations that require effort teach you useful skills and help you grow. Criticism shows you areas where you can improve. Other people's success does not diminish your own, but offers lessons for how you can become more successful, too. New ideas allow you to build on what you know and make it even better.

You can choose to adopt a growth mindset if you don't have one already. Recognizing the difference between these two mindsets is a good first step.

If you accept the premise that your mind can grow and improve with exercise, make sure your outlook matches. When you try something new, you may find yourself automatically reacting with a fixed mindset thought, such as "This looks hard—what if I fail?" or "Oh no, I suck at this, and everyone can see it!" That's ok, just catch yourself and dispute it. Remind yourself that your goal is to grow.

You're learning and practicing and expanding—that is the way to get better, not staying home and acting cool. Choose to see challenges, obstacles, and criticism as opportunities to learn. Stretch yourself by trying new things that you've never done before. This view of the world goes a long way toward getting unstuck and staying unstuck.

Think about...

Do you believe success comes primarily from innate talent and intelligence, or from learning and working hard? Why?

_____

_____

_____

_____

_____

_____

Which of these feel threatening to you?

__ challenges

__ obstacles

__ having to work hard

__ criticism

__ others' success

__ new ideas or approaches

Do you get discouraged when you don't immediately master something?

_____

_____

_____

_____

_____

What would your life be like if you approached everything
with the desire to learn and grow as your primary goal?

_____

_____

_____

_____

_____

_____

_____

_____

_____

_____

_____

_____

_____

_____

_____

_____

_____

_____

Seeing the world with abundance

Another source of stuckness is the need to control everything. Often, the more we try to control things, the more bogged down we get. The need to control comes with a "just in case" mentality—trying to make sure we'll be ok if bad things happen.

The "just in case" mentality stems from the fear that there won't be enough of whatever you need. It's the idea that good things are scarce. Sometimes this is true, but for the most part, there is more than plenty of everything.

It's smart to think ahead and be ready for disaster, but it can waste a lot of resources if you carry it too far. Having some flashlights, a radio, and extra batteries on hand is smart. But if you try to stockpile three months' food and water in case civilization shuts down, that's a lot of money and storage space devoted to canned goods and water instead of something that you could use and enjoy now.

The idea that good things are scarce is a relic from the past. Now, we're surrounded by good things. In fact, one life coach, Martha Beck, phrases it as "Everything good is readily available."[16]

Even if it's not true that *everything* good is readily available, I do believe we get everything we need.

When you believe that, it changes things. If you believe you will get everything you need, you don't have to control everything or worry. After all, if you will get everything you need, what do you have to worry about?

When we believe that everything good is scarce, we can never really feel safe. We always need more money, more things, more love, more food, because there's never enough to counter every "what if?" scenario. Also, when others succeed or get good things, we feel threatened or jealous because we believe that leaves less for us. Even our bodies get into the act by storing fat in case of lean times.

But if we believe that everything good is readily available, we don't have to worry or hoard. All that stuff we're not using can go to other people who need it, because if we need it again later, we can replace it.

We can stop trying to control other people—love them as they are but be ready to let them go if need be—because there is plenty of love available for us.

Some people have even lost weight this way. Given all the fat and sugar that's readily available and almost unavoidable now, about the last thing most of us need to fear is starving to death. Do you hear that, body? You can let go of the belly fat now. We can always get more.

If you find yourself in a scarcity mentality or afraid that you won't be able to get what you need, the first step is to decide you want to change. Even if you don't 100% believe that everything good is readily available, try assuming it for the sake of argument, and see if your life seems more or less pleasant when you filter events through this assumption. I still have a hard time believing it completely, but I've found that just assuming it has made my life more pleasant and eliminated a lot of my worries.

What if I can't do this? You'll get help, or someone else will do it, or it won't get done. No matter what, it will work out ok.

What if I lose my job? You'll get another one or find something else to do for money.

What if I give away this fireplace screen only to have a fireplace again in my next house? You can get a new fireplace screen if that happens. Meanwhile, you can enjoy the space that's not being taken up by something you're not using. The less stuff you have, the less money you need, and the more resources you have to throw at living.

What if I lose my income? You'll find a way to make do with less.

What if I lose my spouse? You can still get love from other sources: family, friends, pets, and maybe even a new romantic relationship someday.

I still have room for improvement in letting go of worry and control, but when I look around, here's what I see: happy people live from the abundance mentality.

You can trigger your own switch to the mentality of abundance by focusing on examples where it has proven true in your own life. How many times have you feared you wouldn't have what you needed but been ok anyway? And how many times have you gotten exactly what you needed when you needed it?

When you let go of your worries and need for control and embrace the abundance mentality, life is freer.

Think about...

Do you believe everything good is readily available?

_____

_____

_____

Do you believe we get everything we need?

_____

_____

_____

Have you ever had a time when you didn't get what you need? If so, how did you make it through?

_____

_____

_____

_____

_____

List ten times when you thought you had too little of something but you survived.

_____

_____

_____

_____

_____

_____

_____

_____

_____

_____

_____

List ten things you have too much of right now.

_____

_____

_____

_____

_____

_____

_____

_____

_____

_____

_____

_____

List ten wonderful things that entered your life at just the right time without effort from you.

_____

_____

_____

_____

_____

_____

_____

_____

_____

_____

How would it feel to let go of "what if"s and trying to control everything, if you knew everything would turn out all right?

_____

_____

_____

_____

_____

_____

_____

Will you try it? If not, what would it take for you to do so?

_____

_____

_____

_____

_____

_____

_____

_____

_____

_____

_____

Moving your body

Exercising can help us get unstuck in two ways.

— When we're stuck, we feel powerless, but when we take action and exercise, it shows we do have some control over our world.

— Sometimes being stuck is related to depression or other mental imbalances. Exercise helps balance the hormones and neurotransmitters in our brains. Research has shown it to be more effective than Zoloft at treating depression and as effective as anti-anxiety drugs at treating anxiety, with no harmful side-effects. What's more, it even stimulates new brain cell growth and helps us learn.[17]

I've never been a big athlete—I know it's important to stay in shape, but not so important that I actually make the time for it. But without intending to, I've done some experiments on myself lately, and it really is amazing what a difference it makes.

I've started running with the Couch to 5k program, and even in weeks 1 and 2, I've noticed that after I run, I can focus and do creative work much longer than usual. Since I started my business, I've also had some times when I was stressed to the max, working as hard as I could, and not taking good care of myself. During those times, I was irritable, prone to despair, tired, and slow. Despite all the action I was taking, I felt powerless and out of control. I felt stuck, even though objectively, I was making tons of progress. The difference between the times when I exercise and the times when I don't is incredible.

It can be hard to get motivated to exercise. I know exercising gives me more energy, but who really believes that when they're tired? It really helps a lot, though, not just with being healthy and getting in shape, but also with mood and being able to think. If you're not convinced, I recommend reading *Spark* by John Ratey.

It's about the amazing effects of exercise on your body and mind, and it blew me away. Health was never enough to motivate me to exercise, but growing new brain cells and being able to focus? I'm there.

Think about...

Do you believe exercise would help you feel better about yourself and your life?

_____

_____

_____

Do you have an exercise routine that you're satisfied with?

_____

_____

_____

What physical activities could you do for fun, rather than focusing on trying to exercise?

_____

_____

_____

_____

_____

_____

_____

_____

Which of these are powerful enough to motivate you to exercise?

__ looking better

__ feeling better

__ being healthy

__ enjoying the activity

__ treating anxiety, depression, ADHD, and others

__ stimulating brain cell growth

__ improved focus

__ a break from the rest of your day

__ doing something for yourself

What physical activity will you do this coming week?

_____

_____

_____

_____

Getting a Running Start

Now that we've explored some of what's behind getting stuck and some tools to help us get out, we're ready to start getting unstuck. For many people, part of the problem is we're not clear on exactly what we want, so we don't really know how to start trying to get there. It reminds me of a quote from *Alice in Wonderland:*

"Would you tell me, please, which way I ought to go from here?"

"That depends a good deal on where you want to get to," said the Cat.

"I don't much care where—" said Alice.

"Then it doesn't matter which way you go," said the Cat.

"—so long as I get SOMEWHERE," Alice added as an explanation.

"Oh, you're sure to do that," said the Cat, "if you only walk long enough."[18]

When you don't really know what you're trying to do, it's hard to get unstuck! Some times in my life I've been certain I knew the answer, and other times I haven't had the slightest clue.

For me, feeling like I'm floundering around in the dark is much more painful than working toward a known goal. When I know what I'm trying to accomplish, everything feels much clearer, and I feel more alive. Even if progress is painfully slow, I can still measure it. It's when I don't know what I'm trying to do or where I'm trying to go that I feel most stuck and hopeless.

Thinking about what you want can be intimidating for two reasons:

— If you know what you want, then you can no longer be content where you are. You have to either take action or continue being dissatisfied.[19]

— We think we have to find the one right answer: our Calling. Most people approach this either by frantically searching through their lives for The One pursuit that will give their lives meaning, or freezing up while hoping the answer will drop out of the sky. Neither of these approaches is every effective for most people—it's better to just wander around and try stuff. If you find something you like, explore it further.[20]

I've spent a lot of time worrying about my grand purpose in life, and it didn't really accomplish much except stress me out. What I've found is that it doesn't really matter if you're wrong. I thought teaching was it for me, and then I thought it was dyeing yarn. Neither of those ended up lasting more than a few years, as it turned out, but the things I learned from both experiences have been really useful for what I'm doing now.

I've let go of trying to find the right answer and started doing stuff for fun. In doing so, I've found something else I really enjoy doing: writing. Now I'm doing that as much as I can. Later, it may fall out of favor and be replaced by something else; that's ok. Our goals and desires change over time as our tastes and our perspective on the world change.

That means you don't have to know the final answer now. There may not even be a final answer. It's ok not to know; you can pick a direction that seems good, set out, and correct your course as you get more information.

Think about...

Do you know where you want to go and what you want to do with your life? Describe it as well as you can.

_____

_____

_____

_____

_____

_____

_____

_____

If you could change the world in any way imaginable, what difference would you want to make?

_____

_____

_____

_____

_____

_____

_____

_____

Figuring out what you really want

If you don't know what you want, here are a few techniques that can help you start figuring it out. We want to know: if you could get out of your rut and have the life of your dreams right now, what would that look like?

For many people, not knowing this is the root of being stuck. Some just can't think of anything good to do. But for many people, the real problem is that what they want seems so hopelessly out of reach, they discount it as a possibility. In many cases, "I don't know what I want" really means "I don't believe I can have what I really want, and I can't think of anything that I want and believe I *can* have."

For now, don't worry about what's possible, just open yourself up to exploration. The "how" will come later.

What's important to you?

One way to start is by exploring your values. When you know what's most important to you, it can help guide you to what you want. On the other hand, if your actions aren't in line with your values, it can cause tension and keep you stuck.

What's most important to you in life? Start by brainstorming. Write your answers down—your ideas will flow more freely if you're not trying to hold them in your head.

It should be pretty easy to come up with a few things; maybe your values include things like honor, learning, prosperity, imagination, and heart. Not all values are easily expressed as just one word; don't worry about that. "Being a good parent" is a fine answer.

If you get stuck, there's a small list of popular values or categories of values in Table 1 (next page)—see if any of them ring a bell for you.

For your list of personal values, coming up with 10 to15 works well—if you have more than that, see if any of them can be combined, or throw out the ones that aren't really that important to you.

Spouse	Taking responsibility
Financial security	Leadership
Personal health and fitness	Inner harmony
Children and family	Independence
A sense of accomplishment	Intelligence and wisdom
Integrity and honesty	Understanding
Occupational satisfaction	Quality of life
Love for others/service	Happiness/positive attitude
Education and learning	Pleasure[21]
Self-respect	

Table 1: Common Values

You may find yourself adding things that you think people *should* value rather than things you actually *do* value. If you catch yourself doing that, take those things out. Nobody's watching. This is your chance to be the real you. That's the only way it works, so be honest.

Once you have a working list of values, take the time to flesh them out a little. If you picked "honor" as a value, what do you mean by that? What will you do to live up to it? Write a sentence or two, or even just some bullet points or phrases, explaining how each one impacts your life.

Next, prioritize. Which of these values is the absolute most important? Rank them in order. It's important to know, not only what you value, but which of those values rank higher than others, because sometimes situations will come up where they're in conflict.

The most obvious example is when someone who values integrity but also values wealth gets an offer to make a lot of money in a dishonest way. That's only a dilemma if you don't know what your values are and how they rank. If you know honesty is the most important thing to you, you'll pass up the offer, but if wealth is most important, you'll take it.[22]

Do you smile at people even though you don't like them? Friendliness must be higher than frankness on your list. Do you stay up late writing, or do you go to bed and get some sleep? Your answer shows whether you value creativity and gratifying work more or less than you value health.

Once you have your values figured out and prioritized, the right decisions for you become clear. But what if you look at your life and find discrepancies between your prioritized values and how you're actually living?

That means something needs to change. Either you don't really value the ones you're violating (so just admit it and redo your list with only your true values), or you really do value them and desperately need to change your actions. This is another deep cause of stuckness, so don't turn a blind eye to any conflicts you spot.

Having your values prioritized also helps with setting goals and deciding which ones to pursue first. If adventure is one of your most important values, maybe your goal of sailing around the world will become your top priority instead of writing a book or saving for retirement. If order is more important to you, maybe you'll choose to do a minimalist purge of your belongings first.

Here's a concrete example. I did this exercise about two years ago and concluded that my top values are integrity, joy, health, creativity, appreciation, connection, growth, and stewardship. Then I clarified them. Some are pretty obvious, but for example, I expanded stewardship as follows:

— Environmental: recycle, eat sustainably, don't waste electricity, etc.

— Time: do the meaningful, valuable things and minimize waste

— People: be kind

For appreciation, I put:
  — Acknowledge and be grateful for the good things in my life

  — Thank people when they help me (on purpose or not)

  — Realize that the events that seem bad are often for my own good and be at peace about them.

Integrity includes:
  — Know my thoughts, needs, wants, likes, dislikes, beliefs, upsets

  — Express these fully in relationships

  — Be truthful in all my dealings

The converse of values is anti-values. Just as your values show you what's important to you, your anti-values show what you find most repellent. If your daily life involves much interaction with your anti-values, that's probably a major contributor to your feeling stuck. Knowing your anti-values can also help you identify what you want by showing you what the opposite looks like.[23]

Some common anti-values are shown in Table 2. Just as you did with your values, rank your anti-values. This time, go in order of what repels you most.

As you look at your list of values and your list of anti-values, compare them with your present life.

Make one more list: things you spend your time on. For most people, this includes eating, sleeping, watching TV, your job, your family obligations, activities with friends, hobbies, and exercise. You may have others, too. List them all.

Now that you have all three lists, you can see how your life fits together. Look at each activity and consider: Which of your values are you supporting when you do it? Are any of your anti-values involved?

Aggression	Fear	Jealousy
Anger	Frivolity	Laziness
Anxiety	Greed	Pain
Apathy	Hate	Pomposity
Arrogance	Hypocrisy	Poverty
Conflict	Ill health	Procrastination
Contempt	Infidelity	Stress
Cynicism	Immorality	Suspicion
Dishonesty	Injustice	Worry[24]
Disgust	Isolation	

Table 2: Common Anti-Values

For example, when I did this exercise, I compared my job with my list of values:

— **Integrity:** No. I felt that I spent a lot of time at work pretending to care about things I didn't really care about, stifling my true feelings, and making myself do things that seemed pointless.

— **Joy:** No. I found most of my time there tedious and mind-numbing.

— **Health:** No. I sat in front of a computer all day. I usually had a headache by the end of the day.

— **Creativity:** Not usually. Occasionally I'd get a task that involved some creativity, but most of it was drudgery.

— **Appreciation:** No. This was my own failure. They didn't appreciate me, and I didn't appreciate them.

— **Connection:** No. The office was like a morgue. Everyone stayed in their own boxes.

— **Growth:** Yes.

— **Stewardship:** No! I felt like I was wasting my life there!

Meanwhile, the office atmosphere often included some of my top anti-values: injustice, anxiety, anger, and jealousy, and I felt the higher-ups were frequently disingenuous, my most-hated form of dishonesty.

Suddenly, I understood why, even though my job was pretty cushy and easy, I hated it so much! I already wanted out, but doing this exercise helped me understand why and reinforced my motivation to change.

On the other hand, my writing hits joy, creativity, connection, and growth directly. It also touches on integrity and appreciation in the subject matter sometimes, and it hits stewardship because I find it a very meaningful use of my time. That's most of my values and none of my anti-values—clearly, this was something to pursue. As you consider what you want out of life, use your values and anti-values to guide you.

What do you enjoy?
It may seem simplistic, but one place to look for what you really want is in what you like. Of the things you do now, what do you enjoy? What other things have you thought about or wished you were doing, but haven't made time for yet? What activities are you drawn to but have never tried? What did you do for fun as a kid?

Don't edit, and don't be practical. Brainstorm a list, and keep writing things down until you have at least 20. Most people get stuck after 7-10—those are the obvious ones. Keep going; you may surprise yourself.

Another exercise that can help is to imagine you've just had a year of your dream life. It was the best year you can imagine, beyond the wildest dreams of your present life. You did anything you wanted, and it all worked even better than you hoped. You're meeting a close friend for lunch, and since this person hasn't seen you for a year, you brought pictures to show what you've been up to.

Mentally flip through the pictures and see them in your mind. What's in the pictures? Who were you with? What were you doing? Where were you?[25]

Again, don't judge, just let your answers flow. They're clues to what you want and what your ideal life would be like.

How do you want to spend your time?

This is the same as asking how you want to spend your life, but somehow it seems easier to think about how we spend our time. You can think of it in smaller pieces, and it's more concrete.

First, think of how you spend your time now. Think about an average week, such as last week. How much time did you devote to sleeping, eating, showering, commuting, errands, work, exercise? What about other things?

How many of those hours are spent on things you enjoy or find meaningful?

Now imagine how you'd like to spend your time. How do you spend your days when you're on vacation? If you didn't have to worry about money or responsibilities and could do anything you wanted, what would your week look like?[26]

How do you want to feel?

As your ideal life starts to take shape in your mind, another thing to consider is how you want to feel. It's probably easy to think of how you *don't* want to feel: anxious, tired, depressed, frustrated, angry...

Thinking of how you do want to feel can be a little less obvious. Think back to some good times you've had. How did you feel? If you were waking up and you somehow knew it was going to be a great day, how would you feel?[27]

Putting it together

Now that we've looked at your values, your anti-values, what you enjoy, how you want to spend your time, and how you want to feel, you may be getting a clearer picture of what you want. Even if you don't have it all figured out, you've probably had a few insights.

You don't have to see the whole picture to get unstuck. Just knowing a few things that would be better will help, because it gives you a direction to go in. Even if you make only the tiniest changes toward what you want and away from what you don't want, it will make a difference. Your life will start feeling better, and you'll feel that you have the power to change it. This is the start of getting unstuck.

Think about...

If you had unlimited resources and could live exactly how you wanted, what would you do? What would your days look like?

_____

_____

_____

_____

_____

What are your top 10-15 values? Make sure you write what you truly value, not what you think you should value or what someone else values. (See the list on page 96 for a starting point.)

_____

_____

_____

_____

_____

_____

_____

_____

_____

_____

For each one, write a few sentences to flesh it out or ex-
plain what you mean by it.

_____

_____

_____

_____

_____

_____

_____

_____

_____

_____

_____

_____

_____

_____

_____

_____

_____

_____

_____

_____

Go back to the list and prioritize them in order of importance.

As you look at your list, does it ring true? Is there anything missing, or anything that doesn't belong?

_____

_____

_____

_____

_____

Thinking about your life, what discrepancies do you see between the way your living and your values and priorities?

_____

_____

_____

_____

_____

_____

_____

_____

_____

_____

_____

What will you do about those discrepancies? Is your list inaccurate, or do you need to change what you're doing?

_____

_____

_____

_____

_____

_____

_____

_____

What are your strongest anti-values? (See page 99.)

_____

_____

_____

_____

_____

_____

_____

_____

_____

Rank your anti-values above in order of how repellent you find them.

In what areas of your life do you experience your anti-values?

_____

_____

_____

_____

_____

What will you do about that?

_____

_____

_____

_____

_____

_____

_____

_____

_____

_____

_____

_____

Getting Unstuck

Make up a schedule showing how you spend your time in a typical week, such as last week.

	Sunday	Monday	Tuesday	Wednesday	Thursday	Friday	Saturday
5:00							
6:00							
7:00							
8:00							
9:00							
10:00							
11:00							
12:00							
1:00							
2:00							
3:00							
4:00							
5:00							
6:00							
7:00							
8:00							
9:00							
10:00							
11:00							
12:00							

What activities did you do, and how much time did you spend on each one?

_____

_____

_____

_____

_____

_____

_____

_____

_____

_____

Which values and anti-values were involved in each activity?

_____

_____

_____

_____

_____

_____

_____

_____

_____

_____

_____

How many hours are spent on things you enjoy or find meaningful?

_____

What do you want to do less of?

_____

_____

_____

_____

What do you want to do more of?

_____

_____

_____

_____

Imagine you've just had a year of the life of your dreams, the best you can possibly imagine. You're about to show your pictures from that year to a friend who hasn't seen you all year, to catch him or her up on what you've been up to. What's in the pictures? Where were you? What did you do? Who were you with?

_____

_____

_____

_____

_____

_____

_____

_____

_____

_____

List 20 things you enjoy doing, did for fun as a kid, or want to try. Brainstorm—don't edit!

_____

_____

_____

_____

_____

_____

_____

_____

_____

_____

_____

Make up a schedule showing how you would spend your time in a typical week of your dream life. If you had no constraints and infinite money, how would you spend your time?

	Sunday	Monday	Tuesday	Wednesday	Thursday	Friday	Saturday
5:00							
6:00							
7:00							
8:00							
9:00							
10:00							
11:00							
12:00							
1:00							
2:00							
3:00							
4:00							
5:00							
6:00							
7:00							
8:00							
9:00							
10:00							
11:00							
12:00							

Compare this schedule with the one from your typical week. What's the same? What's different?

_____

_____

_____

_____

_____

_____

_____

How could you make your real life more like your dream life?

_____

_____

_____

_____

_____

_____

How do you want to feel?

_____

_____

_____

How could you feel that way right now?

_____

_____

_____

_____

_____

_____

How can you feel that way more often?

_____

_____

_____

_____

_____

_____

_____

_____

_____

_____

_____

_____

Gaining Traction

The foundation of getting unstuck is streamlining your mindset. If you're doubting or second-guessing yourself, you become your own biggest obstacle. Here are some techniques to help you.

Erasing limits

This is an amazingly effective technique from Jonathan Mead. Whenever you feel yourself bumping up against internal limitations or feelings that you can't get past, you can use this technique to dissolve the limit and transform it into something that can help you. This is useful before you start something if you're afraid you won't be able to do it, and it's also useful when something is already underway and you find yourself feeling anxious or inadequate.

First, dissolve the limit.

— **Step 1:** Begin with your feeling of discomfort or unwanted limitation. Some examples include not being good enough or not having enough. Give honest thought to the feeling or limitation. Don't judge it or push it away.

— **Step 2:** Once you have a clear awareness of the feeling or thought, allow it to rest. Let it sit within you. Don't resist, just be ok and let it rest.

— **Step 3:** As the feeling rests within you, notice where in your body it's centered. Maybe it's your stomach, your chest, or your head. Maybe it's somewhere else. Allow it to rest in that part of your body, while being gentle with yourself.

— **Step 4:** Keep focusing on the part of your body where the feeling is resting. If thoughts or resistance arise, acknowledge them but return your focus to the part of your body where the feeling is. Keep doing that until the feeling dissolves.

Don't worry about doing it right or wrong—just be patient. There is no right or wrong way to do it and no proper amount of time for it to take.

Once you've dissolved the limit, you can transform it. In fact, you can transform it whether you've dissolved it or not. This process is based on the idea that any unwanted, frustrating, or hindering beliefs have good hidden within them. You can unlock the good parts and leave the hindrance behind.

— **Step 1:** Assume that whatever has been bothering you has some underlying, intended good that you just haven't been able to perceive yet.

— **Step 2:** Look for what the intended good might be for your thought, feeling, or belief. For example, if you're afraid of not having enough money, maybe the underlying good is to protect you from spending too much.

— **Step 3:** Explore further. Keep going deeper and asking yourself what underlies your answers. For example, protection from spending too much money would be keeping you from going broke or going into debt.

— **Step 4:** Keep going deeper until you feel you've reached the root or core and get a sense of finality.

— **Step 5:** Once you've identified the root feeling you're after, ask yourself what it would be like to feel that now. You can feel it right now without having to do anything else—it's available to you. You have everything you need to feel that way already.

— **Step 6:** Tell yourself you want to feel that way. Allow the feeling to flood your consciousness. You don't have to work for it or try to feel that way, you can just feel it. If you have trouble, ask yourself, "Is there _____ even here?" (peace, love, harmony, security, acceptance— whatever your root feeling is)

Continue asking that question and remaining open to whatever arises until you feel the way you want. At that point, you've not only dissolved your limit, you've transformed it into a resource that can help you.[28]

Right after I quit my job, I was very worried about running out of money and not being able to support myself, especially when I wasn't meeting my sales goals and had to incur some unexpected expenses. I felt worried and anxious about it all the time. I know worrying doesn't help anything, so I decided to try this technique.

At first, I felt the worry in the top of my chest, but as I let it rest, it felt rooted in my stomach. In fact, as I felt it there, I realized I had been feeling tense there for weeks.

As I continued to focus my attention on the tension in my stomach, I felt the feeling dissolve. That was an amazing feeling!

After that, I looked for the underlying good. The worry was obviously trying to protect me from going broke. What was under that? Having enough. Being ok. *Feeling secure.*

Could I feel secure now? Was there security even here? Yes! To my surprise, this was a no-brainer. I saved up six months' living expenses before I quit; it was running out later that I was worried about.

I let myself feel secure. I relaxed into the feeling and savored the relief. In addition to feeling better, this experience freed my mind and made it much easier to do my work.

Think about...

Do you have blockages in your mindset, such as self-doubt or second-guessing?

_____

_____

_____

_____

Why do you think that is?

_____

_____

_____

_____

_____

_____

Would you be better off without them?

_____

_____

_____

What limit is holding you back right now?

_____

_____

_____

What underlying good could be at the heart of this hindering belief?

_____

_____

_____

_____

_____

Try the limit-erasing technique described starting on page 115.

What happened?

_____

_____

_____

_____

_____

How do you feel?

_____

_____

_____

_____

_____

_____

_____

Taking it lightly

Many of us believe that anything worth doing will be difficult, and life is meant to be a struggle.

As Lachlan Cotter of The Art of Audacity pointed out on his blog, we often try to motivate ourselves by telling ourselves things like: "I can beat this," "I'll do whatever it takes," "I'm determined," or "I'm in charge."

Although we're on the right track by trying to empower ourselves, the underlying message of all of these statements is "what I'm trying to do is hard." Otherwise, why would you have to do whatever it takes or be so determined?

Another possibility is to think about how it could be fun or easy. Rather than seeing what you're doing as an intimidating thing, how could you take it (and yourself) less seriously? How could you see it as an experiment?[29]

That's a big one for me. When I'm considering starting something, if it seems serious, I have a hard time making myself do it. It seems like a huge commitment to a bunch of drudgery.

I often feel like if I start something, then I'll either be stuck doing it forever or be a quitter—those are the only two options. But that's not really true. If you're just trying something to see what it's like, then the stakes are low. If you don't like it, no biggie. If you don't follow it with slavish devotion, no worries. That was never the plan. If you happen to like it, then great! But if not, you just try something else.

For example, I'm trying this approach with learning to play the cigar box guitar, and it's working really well.

Growing up, I played a few different instruments, and I was pretty good. I enjoyed playing in the band or the orchestra, but I rarely played on my own just for fun. It always seemed like a chore. The only way I'd practice was if I was trying to get ready for a solo or challenging for a higher chair. I felt I should be the best, and I was often first chair, but I did it with as little effort as I thought I could get away with.

The cigar box guitar is totally different. I bought one on a whim because they seemed easy to pick up. I wanted to play folky classic rock songs for myself to sing along to.

That's it. I don't intend to join a band or play in front of anyone else. I don't care if I'm good or if I'm doing it right. I don't practice. I don't memorize scales or chord charts. I just play because it's fun and I like singing. Ironically, I end up picking it up almost every day, not because I have a goal, just because I enjoy it so much.

I started my blog with the same approach as the cigar box guitar: just trying it to see how I liked it, no commitments or expectations. Starting with that mindset takes a lot of pressure off.

Think about...

When you take on a challenge, what do you tell yourself?

_____

_____

_____

_____

_____

What could you tell yourself instead, that would be motivational but not intimidating?

_____

_____

_____

_____

_____

Think about something you're stuck on now.

Why do you want to do it?

_____

_____

_____

_____

_____

If you have tension or a feeling of obligation, how can you see it as your choice instead of something you "have to" do?

_____

_____

_____

_____

_____

_____

How could you see it as fun, easy, or experimental?

_____

_____

_____

_____

_____

_____

_____

_____

_____

_____

_____

Believing in yourself

When you believe in yourself, you stop fighting against yourself and join your own team. But how can you believe in yourself if you don't now?

One way to start is to gather evidence and prove to yourself that you can succeed. If you've been in the habit of thinking of yourself as a loser or a failure, now is the time to change that. Think back through the goals you've achieved in the past. No matter where you are now, there has to be at least one goal you've achieved, probably more. What were they?

For each goal, write down why you made that goal, how you achieved it, and what carried you through achieving it. Why did you succeed? What made the difference?[30]

Examine them closely, and be thorough. Look for patterns of how you succeeded—those will help you achieve future goals. But more importantly, look at how much you've achieved. Think back to how you felt when you set each goal, and how far off the end seemed. Then remember how it felt when you succeeded. You can do that again—you still have those abilities within you.

It also helps to stop comparing yourself with others. It's hard to believe in yourself when you look around and see people who seem so confident, successful, and perfect. The trap there is you're comparing your insides to their outsides. You know all of your weaknesses, fears, and struggles. For them, all you see is the polished exterior and the finished product, not what's going on inside or what it took to get where they are.[31]

Comparisons like that are unfair and make you feel worse without accomplishing anything. Let them go, focus on yourself, and believe in yourself.

Think about...

What goals have you achieved in the past? Write down as
many successes and achievements as you can think of.

_____

_____

_____

_____

_____

_____

_____

_____

_____

_____

_____

_____

_____

_____

_____

_____

_____

_____

_____

_____

_____

_____

_____

_____

_____

For each of your top 3 goals, answer these questions:

Goal 1

Why did you set this goal?

_____

_____

_____

_____

What struggles and obstacles did you face?

_____

_____

_____

_____

Did you ever feel like giving up? What made you keep going?

_____

_____

_____

_____

How did you achieve it—what carried you through? What made the difference?

_____

_____

_____

_____

_____

How did it feel to achieve success? Think back and experience that feeling again.

_____

_____

_____

_____

_____

_____

_____

_____

Goal 2

Why did you set this goal?

_____

_____

_____

_____

_____

_____

_____

What struggles and obstacles did you face?

_____

_____

_____

_____

Did you ever feel like giving up? What made you keep going?

_____

_____

_____

_____

_____

_____

How did you achieve it—what carried you through? What made the difference?

_____

_____

_____

_____

_____

How did it feel to achieve success? Think back and experience that feeling again.

_____

_____

_____

_____

_____

_____

_____

_____

Goal 3

Why did you set this goal?

_____

_____

_____

_____

What struggles and obstacles did you face?

_____

_____

_____

_____

Did you ever feel like giving up? What made you keep going?

_____

_____

_____

_____

_____

How did you achieve it—what carried you through? What made the difference?

_____

_____

_____

_____

_____

_____

How did it feel to achieve success? Think back and experience that feeling again.

_____

_____

_____

_____

_____

_____

_____

Looking at these success stories from your life, what patterns do you see?

_____

_____

_____

_____

_____

_____

_____

_____

_____

Do you believe your current struggles could be similar, with success waiting on the other side?

_____

_____

_____

_____

How can you apply the patterns of your past successes to your current endeavors?

_____

_____

_____

_____

_____

_____

_____

_____

_____

_____

_____

_____

_____

_____

Taking Action

> **"**If you only do two things—take consistent action and lose your fear of failure—you'll already have a 95% chance of success.**"**
>
> —Jonathan Mead[32]

Commitment

When you take on a new challenge, it's easy to be daunted by how far you are from where you want to be. You may waste a lot of time vacillating about whether to even try. Can you do it? Can't you do it? Will it all be a huge waste of effort? What if it doesn't work?

Wouldn't it be nice if you already knew the outcome in advance? If you already knew how things will turn out, you could just go straight to your goal without worrying or second-guessing.

We can't see into the future, but we can influence it with our attitudes and actions. What if you decided to act as if your desired outcome is a foregone conclusion? You know you will do it, you will get there, you will achieve your goal.

If you want something badly enough, it's worth committing to. Decide you're going to do it—it *will* happen.

From there, it's no longer a matter of "Can I do this?"—it's "How will I do this?" When something unexpected gets in the way, you don't have to think "Should I keep going, or quit?" All you have to think about is how you'll overcome it. Roadblocks are just obstacles to overcome. Setbacks are no cause for despair, they just add interest and drama to the story you'll tell at your victory party.

This shift helped me immensely when I decided I wanted to support myself as a writer and quit my job. I had a blog with a very small audience, but I didn't seem to be making any visible progress, and I wasn't sure I'd ever be able to stand on my own. In fact, I had a few other ideas for making money that seemed more likely to succeed.

However, when I joined a six-month coaching program that promised to get me to the point where I could quit my job, I stopped doubting or guessing. I stopped thinking about whether I could do it. I just put myself in my coach's hands and got to work doing whatever he said. He seemed to think I could do it, and he was the expert, so I left him to worry about how to make it happen.

By the end of the program, I still wasn't sure whether I was quite ready to quit immediately, but I was sure I'd have a sustainable income stream within six more months at the latest. I had enough to live on until then, so I quit my job and struck out on my own.

When you commit to doing something and stop doubting that you can do it, you are powerful beyond measure. If you really throw yourself into it, you can make it happen. Everything won't go as planned, and it may not follow your exact timeline, but those things don't really matter in the face of doing what you want. I feel incredibly lucky to be living my dream life. It's not perfect, but it is fabulous.

Taking your desired outcome as a given can save you a lot of thinking, worrying, second-guessing, and re-deciding. It can also change your attitude about yourself. Instead of wondering if you're good enough or seeing yourself as unworthy of others who have already achieved your goal, you start to see yourself as a victor in the making. You're the same as them; it's just a matter of time until you get where they are now.

I made this shift in the early days of building my business. I used to be very intimidated by established bloggers. I didn't think they'd want to talk to me because I was just little me with my tiny blog and my audience of 17, whereas they were Successful Big Deal People, read by thousands and admired far and wide.

My coach, Jonathan Mead, stopped me in my tracks with this line of reasoning. He said that successful people can tell who's on the way. They recognize them as their own kind, just lacking a few months.

What he said rang true. When I used to teach, I could tell which students were on the path to success and which ones were off in the weeds. And all that was standing between me and success was knowing what to do (which I'd hired Jonathan for) and doing it (which I knew I would). I had been around long enough to see a few others go from releasing their first products to being well known and making a lot of money within a year or two. I could do that, too.

That realization shifted my thinking. Instead of thinking of myself as a wanna-be, a moonlighter, or a cubicle slave, I started thinking of myself as a successful blogger who just lacked a few months. That mental shift gave me a lot more confidence, and when I ran into people who didn't respect me, instead of cowering back into my cave, I got indignant and predicted how stupid they would feel later when they realized how much they had underestimated me.

Some people also say that this kind of thinking creates a gap between reality and your self-image that makes your mind really uncomfortable, so it hustles to make you awesome to close the gap.[33] I don't know how true that is, but if it's real, it's a great bonus!

Once you've decided you care about something enough to do it, treat it as something important in your life. Sometimes it seems like the closer something is to our essential selves, the more readily we allow it to be pushed aside. That's not cool. If something is important to you, *it's important!*

Don't call your dreams "my silly little…" or "oh, that's just my… " Don't say "I hope someday…" Whatever you're doing, even when you're just starting out, is real and worthy of respect.

I think a lot of people, myself included, are afraid of coming across as arrogant or foolish if we say things like "I'm a writer, and I'm going to support myself doing work I love!" or "I'm writing now, so I'm not available to answer the phone or do anything else," instead of "I have a little blog, and I'm trying to do this thing, but I don't really know what I'm doing…" or "[This was meant to be my writing time, but] sure, I'll run an errand for you."

Maybe it's shyness or excessive humility, or maybe it's some old superstition: don't brag or you'll draw the evil spirits' attention. Whatever it is, it needs to go! Your dreams and your beloved pursuits are some of your best stuff. Make them a priority, nurture them, and invest in them. Don't discount them or push them aside. Live them and fulfill them!

Think about...

If consistent action is the number one determining factor in success, what does that mean for you?

_____

_____

_____

_____

_____

_____

_____

What's most important to you to work toward at this time in your life?

_____

_____

_____

_____

_____

Do you want it enough to commit to working on it regularly?

_____

Are you ready to let go of wondering and doubting, and instead determine that it _will_ happen?

_____

How does that change your thinking?

_____

_____

_____

_____

_____

What will you do when you encounter setbacks and things that don't go as planned?

_____

_____

_____

_____

_____

How can you treat this endeavor as something valued and important in your life?

_____

_____

_____

_____

_____

_____

Getting started

Many people struggle with getting started. We have great ideas, but we never get around to pursuing them. Whether it's because we're intimidated, we don't make time, or we're afraid we're unworthy to take on such pursuits, stuckness abounds.

For me, the hardest part of almost everything I do is getting started. It's the part I dread the most, and it's the part that's hardest to make myself do. In my case, there are two factors involved:

— The blank slate of a new project can be overwhelming. I have a much easier time when I feel like I have a clear understanding of what's involved and what I need to do, and you almost never have that before getting started.

— "Eat, drink, and be merry, for tomorrow we diet" syndrome. I have a lot of big ideas, and I know that once I start something, it will take up a lot of my life. Either I'll be working on it, or I'll be feeling bad about not having worked on it. So I tend to have one last fling in my life as a free person... and then another, and another. Even when I sit down for a work session, I do the same thing. I want to write, but suddenly I realize I have a hangnail, and my glasses are dirty, and I should really refill my water mug before I get too absorbed... Even though I love being absorbed in a project, I do this little dance of delay to keep it from happening.

Another reason we have a hard time starting things is that we get stuck trying to find the perfect way to start. We don't want to have to backtrack, so we hesitate and get stuck in analysis paralysis. In reality, we usually have no way of knowing what the best way to start will be, because we don't know enough about the project yet. So instead of just starting *somewhere,* we freeze.

How to get started getting started

The great thing about starting being the hardest part is that once you've done it, everything else is easier! What's more, getting started is binary. Either you've started, or you haven't. You don't have to do something huge or intimidating, you just have to do *something.*

To pry myself out to my resistance to starting, I like to remove some of the mystery from the project. When something is hazy and undefined, I lack confidence that I can do it. But when I see clearly what's involved, I often get excited about what I'm doing and *want* to start.

My favorite way to gain clarity is to break the project down until I understand it. I start by summarizing what I'm trying to accomplish in a sentence or two. Then I list, at a very high level, what steps I'll need to take to get there. Then I start breaking down the steps within each step. I keep breaking things down until I have a list of tasks that I understand and could do in no more than a few days apiece.

For example, when I first heard about publishing in the Kindle Store, I wanted to try it, but I really didn't know how to go about it.

Summary: Publish at least four short pieces to the Kindle store by December 15.

High-level steps:
- Find out what's involved
- Write or repurpose content
- Turn each piece into an ebook
- Put them in the Kindle store
- Promote them.

Break it down one level:
- Find out what's involved

- — Amazon website: what's the commission structure?
- — Forums: what has worked best for others?
- — Amazon website: what do I actually need to do to get my stuff into the right format and on the site?
— Write or repurpose content
   - — Look through old stuff and see if I have anything I could reuse
   - — If not, write new stuff
   - — Edit
— Turn each piece into an ebook
   - — Come up with a title
   - — Design a cover or pay someone to do it
   - — Do layout or pay someone to do it
   - — Convert to .mobi format or pay someone to do it
— Put them in the kindle store
   - — Upload the files
   - — Whatever else is involved?
— Promote them
   - — Twitter
   - — Facebook
   - — Email
   - — Blog

From there, I would keep breaking down anything that still seemed too complex to be one task. I would also need to resolve the question mark items. But even with the murky areas, this feels much clearer than when I started.

By this point, usually one or two tasks stand out as something I'd like to get on right away, or something that I could easily knock out. I pick one of those and do it, and voila! I've started!

Think about...

Do you find yourself intimidated by the blank slate of a new project?

_____

_____

_____

Do you put off starting to keep your life the same a little bit longer?

_____

_____

_____

What's something you're currently having a hard time start-ing?

_____

_____

_____

_____

What can you learn that would help you feel more equal to this task or project?

_____

_____

_____

_____

_____

What are you trying to accomplish, in 1-3 sentences?

_____

_____

_____

_____

_____

What high-level steps will you need to take to accomplish that?

_____

_____

_____

_____

_____

_____

_____

_____

_____

_____

_____

_____

_____

_____

What steps will you need to do to complete each of those high-level steps?

_____

_____

_____

_____

_____

_____

_____

_____

_____

_____

_____

_____

_____

_____

_____

_____

_____

_____

_____

_____

_____

_____

_____

_____

_____

_____

_____

_____

_____

_____

_____

Do you know how to do each of those steps? If not, keep breaking them down until you feel like you have a handle on what's involved at each step, even if you don't yet have all the knowledge you need to complete them all. (Use extra paper if you need to.)

As you look at the list of steps, what task seems appealing or doable right now?

_____

_____

When will you do it?

_____

_____

How to keep going

Once you've started, it's much easier to keep going. Just look at your task list, pick one small task, and do it. When you've finished that, pick another and do it. Keep looking for one small step that will get you closer to your goal, and taking that step. As you do that over and over, you make progress. You don't have to worry about which one is the best step to take next; often it doesn't matter. Just pick one that looks appealing or easy, and do it.

If you find yourself trying to do things but continually having to go back and do something else first, you've found a situation where the order does matter. In that case, to save yourself time and frustration, go back to your list of tasks. For each one, break it down further by writing everything that needs to be completed before you can do it. You may have to build yourself a flow chart, or you may be able to simply start with the prerequisites, do them, and then do the task.

This may seem simplistic, but really, all it takes to achieve a goal is knowing what needs to be done, and doing it. If you keep making progress toward your goal, eventually, you will get there.

To stay motivated as you keep working, you may find it helpful to monitor your progress. If there are statistics or metrics you can use, that's great. For example, when I started my blog, my Alexa rank was over 5 million. (That means Alexa ranked over 5 million sites on the internet as more significant than mine.) But as the weeks went by, that number got lower and lower. Now I'm around 660,000. It's an arbitrary number, but watching it move helped me feel like I was getting somewhere—it was like a nod of approval from the internet itself.

Better than that is a metric you have more direct control over. Depending on your project, there may be something that naturally fits, or you may pick something simple like the number of tasks you've accomplished so far. For me, making it visual is even more powerful. I'll write out the task list in all its detailed glory, and then rejoice as I check things off. As those checkmarks accumulate, I can see how much I've done and how much I have left.

Seeing that I'm making progress helps me feel good about what I'm doing and stay motivated. If you're less of a checkmark nerd, find some other way to monitor your progress that's meaningful for you.

Think about...

What step will you take next to make progress on your most important projects or goals?

_____

_____

How will you monitor your progress?

_____

_____

_____

_____

What metrics could you apply?

_____

_____

_____

_____

_____

How could you represent your progress visually?

_____

_____

_____

_____

What to do if you get bogged down

As you continue working on your project, you may find yourself stagnating. You may find it difficult to focus or stay motivated. This can happen even on a project that means a lot to you. I've found a few techniques that help when that happens.

Take a step back

When you're stuck on a project, pause and think. Where exactly are you stuck? What are you trying to do? Why can't you do it? What do you need?

If the problem is more that you just can't make yourself get to work, ask yourself why? Are you afraid you'll screw up? Confused? Intimidated?

Think back. Why did you start this project in the first place? What would it accomplish? How would it help you or others? Do you still find that a compelling reason to keep going?

If you're no longer convinced the project is worth doing, then feel free to drop it. However, if you still have compelling reasons for doing it, hang onto them and use them to draw you forward.

Most things worth doing have what Seth Godin calls The Dip: the period after the novelty wears off and things start getting tough. As you slog along, you feel like you'll never get there. But if you stick it out, things turn around and you start seeing a lot of results fast. Making it through The Dip is what separates the successful from the also-rans, so unless you're on a dead-end effort and seeing no measurable progress for your labors, keep pushing through.[34]

Structured Decision-Making

When the problem is intimidation or confusion, applying a structured process to problem-solving can help. One process I like is called GROW:

  — **Goal**—what you want to do,

— **Reality**—the current situation or your perception of it,

— **Options**—Possible ways to get from the current reality to the goal,

— **Way Forward**—which action you will take.

The first step is **Goal:** remember what you're trying to do. Make sure you're clear on that. Has it shifted since you started?

Next, **Reality:** describe the current situation. What have you tried so far? How's it going? What's working? What's not? What results have you gotten?

Then, **Options:** brainstorm possible approaches. Don't discount ideas, even if they're silly or infeasible. Just think up as many possibilities as you can.

Finally, the **Way Forward:** Evaluate the options and decide what you will do next.

By using this structured approach, you can clarify your thinking, focus, and take a direct route to finding a solution.[35]

Focus in short total-immersion sessions
When I'm squirmy or squirrelly, the thought of the big picture or a whole afternoon of work is enough to send me running for Facebook. If you get into the habit of running from your work and immersing yourself in distractions, it can get very difficult to focus and get anything done.

I had a huge problem with this for a while at my old job. I didn't really care about anything I was supposed to be working on anyway, and it was hard, and I didn't want to do it. I found it almost impossible to make myself do any work, and even when I miraculously got myself to start something, I'd be off chasing butterflies in a matter of minutes. I was convinced I had ADD and would never work in computer science again. This technique saved my bacon. It's the only way I got myself to work.

Pick one task that you need to do. Tell yourself you'll just work on it for 20 minutes, and then you can take a break. Then stick with it!

The traditional method is to use a timer, but you can also just note your starting time. Before you start, eliminate as many distractions as you can. Turn off your email notifications, close websites and applications you don't need for this task, close your office door. Then set the timer and start working.

The key is, don't stop until the 20 minutes are up, no matter what! If you're like me, you'll think of a million things you need to research that have nothing to do with your task. Do not research them. Just note them on a scrap of paper; you can get to them later. Focus only on the task at hand.

If you find yourself tempted by distractions, check the timer. Tell yourself "Only X minutes left, and then I can take a break," and direct your attention back to the task at hand. This may seem like torture at first, but as you practice, it gets easier. Stick with it for the entire 20 minutes. When time is up, reward yourself with a break and/or some other small treat. When you're ready, set the timer and start another session.

The great thing about this technique is that even in one 20-minute session, if you focus on what you're doing, you can get some traction and make a little bit of progress. That feels good and shows you that you can do this, which makes it easier to go on and do more.

If you're as mentally out of shape as I was, you may only be able to do two or three sessions on your first day. That's ok. You can build up over the coming days. Working like this retrains your attention span and conditions you to focus on your work, which is crucial for accomplishing things.

Over time, you may find yourself so into what you're doing that you run over the 20-minute block. That's ok. In fact, that's fabulous! Work in the flow state, when you get absorbed in the work and lose track of the world around you, is the ultimate. It feels great, and the work produced is high quality. Take advantage of it when you can.[36]

Just make sure you give yourself a break when you surface. Taking a good break will help you concentrate again in your next session, and it's important to be able to count on yourself to keep your word. If you say you'll take a break or get some other reward, but then you don't give it to yourself, it will be that much harder to motivate yourself next time.

The Unschedule

Sometimes, we get bogged down because we can't live up to our own expectations, and all we see is more work ahead. This technique helps with both problems.

When we think about how long we expect something to take, we often fail to take into account all the other things we'll be doing during the same time period. For example, a work week may seem plenty long enough to write a report... until you factor in all of the time you'll spend on meetings, conference calls, email, and your other projects. Considering how much time those things take, three weeks might not be enough time to finish the report.

Furthermore, if all we see coming is one long stream of work, it seems pointless to worry too much about finishing any one thing. If it will just be replaced with more work as soon as you finish it, why bother?

An unschedule can help combat both of these perceptions. An unschedule looks like a schedule at first glance, but instead of filling in your tasks and when you plan to work, you block off all of the time that is unavailable for work. As you map out your week, block off the time you spend eating, sleeping, commuting, showering, running errands, going to meetings, and any other commitment that takes your time.

To counter the perception that life is only work, also block off time for some activities you enjoy. This could be going out dancing, time with friends, watching a movie, or simply taking some alone time. Block that time off. To add impact, you may even mark it in a different color so that you have an obvious visual representation showing that there will be fun coming up and life is not all work.

Once you've done that, look at the time that's left. It looks far less than "a week" sounds, doesn't it? Looking at that, your history of accomplishing less than you hoped probably makes a lot more sense.

The final trick with the unschedule is to write in work only *after* you've done it. Each time you do a session of uninterrupted work, record it on your unschedule. Record the other things you do, too, so you can see where you're spending your time. At the end of the week, you can see your work time in perspective with all of your other commitments.

As you do this over time, you can also see patterns of when you're most productive and when you're least productive. If you schedule your less productive times with the tasks that are easy or less important and save your best times for your most demanding work, you'll be more efficient. Meanwhile, just seeing a true picture of your constraints and seeing fun on the horizon can help a lot.[37]

Other tips

Here are some more tips to help when you get bogged down.

- Lighten up on your expectations. Nobody is perfect, and you can't do it all in one day.

- Don't get stuck trying to find the perfect solution. Do your research, find a good way, and do it. If you're doing something no one else has done before, you may not even know what's a good way and what's not until you try, so try something. If that doesn't work, try something else.

— As you gather more information, you'll be able to pick a solution that works. Most problems have many possible solutions that will work. It's better to pick something and get started than to stay stuck. You can do a course correction later if you need to.

— Remember how crappy you feel when you don't accomplish anything and how great you feel when you do. Use that to motivate yourself to get to work.

— Don't think about finishing the whole daunting project. Just think of one thing you can do to get started, the simpler the better. Look at your list of small doable steps and do the easiest one. The feeling of success you'll get from accomplishing that will help you face the next.

— Don't try to do a marathon. Just do one small piece and take a break.

— Don't try to make up for all the time you've already lost. You can't go back and unprocrastinate, and you can't do all those days' work (and today's!) today. It's impossible, and the more you think about it, the more you'll psych yourself out. Just let it go and start from today.

— Don't be afraid to do imperfect work. Your work won't be perfect the first time, and that's ok. If you just get something down, you can improve it later. It's much easier to take something mediocre and make it good than to take nothing and make something.

— Whenever you catch yourself making excuses or claiming you can't do entire categories of tasks, disprove the statement by finding times when you have done those things, and done them well.

— Make yourself accountable to someone. At my job, I reported to my boss every Friday on what I'd accomplished that week. Some weeks, I hated it, because I'd be scrambling on Friday to get something accomplished so I'd have something to report. Some weeks I had nothing and embarrassedly sugar-coated this fact. But it made me way more productive—knowing I had to report in spurred me to try to finish something every week.

— Embrace choice. A wise friend once told me that no matter who's paying you, you're always working for yourself. Ultimately, you are the one you have to satisfy.

I think that's true, and it can also be flipped around: if you work for yourself, you have a choice as to whether you do any of these tasks or not. Just because your boss assigns you a user guide to edit or a piece of code to write, it doesn't mean you actually have to do it. It's your choice. You can do a great job, you can do a so-so job, you can act like you did it but really not do it, or you can just refuse to do it.

Some of these possibilities may get you bad reviews or eventually fired, but that doesn't mean you don't have a choice. If you do the task, it's because you're choosing to do it, even if only because it's better than getting fired. That's a powerful thing to remember. Choose to do things, or choose not to do them, and know that's what you're doing. Then refuse to let your excuses stop you.

Think about...

What projects are you bogged down on?

_____

_____

_____

_____

_____

_____

_____

Where exactly are you stuck?

_____

_____

_____

_____

_____

_____

What are you trying to do?

_____

_____

_____

_____

_____

_____

Why can't you do it?

_____

_____

_____

What have you tried do far? What's working? What's not?

_____

_____

_____

_____

_____

_____

_____

_____

_____

What results have you gotten so far?

_____

_____

_____

_____

_____

What would help you do it? (Ex. More information, inspiration, an outside opinion, help)

_____

_____

_____

_____

_____

_____

What are you afraid of?

_____

_____

_____

_____

_____

_____

_____

Why did you start this project in the first place?

_____

_____

_____

_____

What benefits will you and others experience if you ac-complish it?

_____

_____

_____

_____

_____

_____

_____

_____

_____

_____

_____

Do you still believe it's worth doing?

_____

_____

Are you in The Dip, or is it a dead-end effort? What evi-dence supports this assessment?

_____

_____

_____

_____

_____

Will you press on and continue working, or drop the project and move on to something else?

_____

If you're continuing the project, brainstorm: What possible approaches can you think of to get you closer to your goal on this project?

_____

_____

_____

_____

_____

_____

_____

_____

_____

_____

_____

_____

_____

_____

_____

Which of these options seems best? Why?

_____

_____

_____

_____

_____

_____

What will you do next?

_____

_____

_____

Do you have a hard time focusing on your projects or tasks long enough to be productive?

_____

_____

Try a 20-minute total immersion session—turn off all distractions and don't let yourself stray from your task until the 20 minutes are up. Then take a break.

How did you feel during the 20 minutes?

_____

_____

_____

_____

_____

How did you feel after?

_____

_____

_____

_____

_____

What are the benefits of working this way?

_____

_____

_____

_____

_____

If it gets easier over time, do you think this technique could help you feel better about yourself and be more productive? Why or why not?

_____

_____

_____

_____

Will you do it more?

_____

_____

Draw up your unschedule for the coming week. Block off all of the time that you'll need for sleeping, eating, commuting, grooming, appointments, meetings, fun times, and social obligations.

	12:00	11:00	10:00	9:00	8:00	7:00	6:00	5:00	4:00	3:00	2:00	1:00	12:00	11:00	10:00	9:00	8:00	7:00	6:00	5:00
Sunday																				
Monday																				
Tuesday																				
Wednesday																				
Thursday																				
Friday																				
Saturday																				

What fun things do you have to look forward to in this week?

_____

_____

_____

_____

_____

_____

_____

How much usable working time do you have available?

_____

_____

How does it compare to the amount you imagine yourself having in a week?

_____

_____

_____

_____

_____

_____

_____

_____

List the tasks you would like to accomplish in the next week. For each one, estimate how many hours it will take you.

_____

_____

_____

_____

_____

_____

_____

_____

_____

_____

_____

_____

_____

_____

_____

_____

_____

_____

_____

_____

_____

Don't schedule tasks onto your unschedule; just compare the total hours of work with the total hours available for work. Do you have enough time available this week to accomplish everything you want?

_____

Knowing that nobody actually fills all of the available work time with work, how will you adjust your expectations for what you get done this week?

_____

_____

_____

_____

_____

_____

What tasks will give you the most payoff or progress toward your goals?

_____

_____

_____

_____

_____

_____

How will you order your tasks to ensure you accomplish those?

_____

_____

_____

_____

_____

_____

_____

How can you give yourself small wins and minimize the intimidation factor of your to-do list?

_____

_____

_____

_____

_____

_____

_____

Do you often find yourself feeling behind and trying to do an impossible amount of work in attempt to catch up?

_____

_____

Can you let go of everything you haven't accomplished up to now and start from this moment?

_____

_____

_____

Who could help you stay accountable for what you want to accomplish?

_____

_____

_____

_____

Conquering Procrastination

When you're stuck on a project, procrastination is likely. Most people think people procrastinate because we're lazy. As we saw earlier, many people believe humans would never do anything if left to our own devices, and it's only discipline and consequences that make us do anything.

That may be true in some situations, but we're happier when we're accomplishing things. The flow state is one of the most abundant sources of deep satisfaction and happiness in the world. If we were inherently lazy, there wouldn't be so many people who use their free time to think, write, learn, invent, or create.

Procrastination is a way we hold ourselves back, but it doesn't mean we're stupid or lazy. It means we've been conditioned by our experiences to believe it will get us something we want.

When we procrastinate, we receive an immediate reward: the removal of tension, and the comfort of doing something easier or safer. Procrastination protects us from some of our deepest fears: the fear of being imperfect, the fear of impossible expectations, and the fear of failure. If your self-worth is tied up in your accomplishments, procrastination is all the more appealing as an escape from these fears.

If you fear imperfection, putting off a task until the last minute gives you a built-in excuse. If the work isn't good enough, it's not a reflection of your true abilities—you could have done much better given more time. Meanwhile, if you have a fear of success, it helps there, too: nobody can resent you for being too successful if you never finish your project. That also guards against criticism—as long as you haven't finished, it's still a work in progress, so you're safe from judgment.

We also use procrastination as a form of quiet rebellion. Your boss may require you to do this report, but he can't make you do it *now!*

On top of that, many times procrastination is rewarded. The

task you didn't want to do gets canceled or done by someone else; the test you didn't study for gets postponed due to a snow day; the decision you were stuck on gets resolved on its own as one of your choices disappears. These reprieves don't happen all the time, but they happen often enough to reinforce procrastination roulette as an option that sometimes pays off.[38]

When you consider all of these factors, it's not so surprising that we procrastinate. It's a behavior with a track record of paying off in various ways. When we procrastinate, it's because the immediate rewards it offers are more appealing than the reward of doing our work. To overcome procrastination, we need to make the reward of doing a task more enticing than the reward of putting it off. Planning a treat for yourself at the end of the task and envisioning how great you'll feel when you've accomplished your goal are good ways to start. Techniques such as the Unschedule and Short Total-Immersion sessions help, too.

You can also shift the balance by removing some of the dread or intimidation from doing the work, so you won't feel such a strong desire to put it off. As we've seen, a lot of stuckness comes from how we interpret a situation. When you're thinking about your projects,

— **Replace "I have to" with "I choose to."** Remember, you have a choice, and you have the final say on whether you do something or not. If you choose to do it, claim your power and own it.

— **Replace "I must finish" with "When can I start?"** Focusing on finishing encourages you to feel intimidated, overwhelmed, anxious, and filled with despair. Instead, focus on the next small step you will take and when you will take it. That's how you make progress.

— **Replace "This is so big" with "I can take one small step."** Again, don't let yourself get overwhelmed. Focus on the one thing you will do next to get a little closer to your goal.

— **Replace "I must be perfect" with "I can be human."** Nobody is perfect. Don't expect yourself to be, and don't beat yourself up when you're not.

— **Replace "I don't have time to play" with "I must take time to play."** Breaks and recreation help us enjoy life. They also make us more productive in the long run.[39]

As you change your thinking, you can release many of the thought patterns that keep you overwhelmed and trigger procrastination. By continuing to redirect yourself to the next small step and acting to take that step, you will overcome procrastination.

Think about...

Do you think of yourself as a lazy person, or fear you might be?

_____

_____

_____

_____

What do you do for fun, even though it requires effort?

_____

_____

_____

_____

_____

How do you feel when in the moment when you do something else instead of a task you don't want to do?

_____

_____

_____

_____

_____

_____

_____

How do you feel later?

_____

_____

_____

_____

_____

_____

_____

_____

Which of these fears do you identify with?

__ fear of being imperfect

__ fear of impossible expectations

__ fear of failure

__ fear of criticism

__ fear of success

How might you be using procrastination as a form of rebellion or self-expression?

_____

_____

_____

_____

_____

_____

List five incidents when procrastination paid off—you put something off, and then it didn't need to be done after all, or the deadline was postponed.

_____

_____

_____

_____

_____

_____

How can you relax your feelings of overwhelm and intimidation, and start on your task?

_____

_____

_____

_____

_____

_____

_____

_____

_____

_____

What rewards can you use to entice yourself?

_____

_____

_____

_____

_____

How will you make sure you take care of yourself and get
enough time for fun?

_____

_____

_____

_____

_____

_____

_____

_____

_____

_____

_____

_____

_____

Conclusion

> **"** Remembering that I'll be dead soon is the most important tool I've ever encountered to help me make the big choices in life. Because almost everything— all external expectations, all pride, all fear of embarrassment or failure—these things just fall away in the face of death, leaving only what is truly important. Remembering that you are going to die is the best way I know to avoid the trap of thinking you have something to lose. You are already naked. There is no reason not to follow your heart. **"**
>
> — Steve Jobs[40]

This quote from Steve Jobs was inspirational before his death and is even more poignant now. We spend so much time and energy worrying about the inconsequential and the unlikely. Don't waste your life that way. Step out. Take the risk. Act.

Not everything will turn out as you hope, but that's ok. Learn, correct your course, and keep acting. You don't have to know what you're doing, and you won't know all the answers. Do it anyway. Try. Risk. Grow. *Live.*

Think about...

At the end of your life, what do you want to look back on and have others remember you for?

_____

_____

_____

_____

_____

_____

_____

_____

_____

_____

_____

How do you think the fears you have now will seem to you then?

_____

_____

_____

_____

_____

_____

Think back to what you were afraid of or worried about ten years ago.

How much of it do you remember?

_____

_____

_____

_____

_____

How important does it seem now?

_____

_____

_____

_____

_____

What one small action can you take to get you a tiny bit closer to your goals and dreams?

_____

_____

When will you do it?

_____

_____

Congratulations!

You did the whole thing! That's a serious investment you've made in yourself. Pat yourself on the back and do something to celebrate. You deserve it!

Want more?

If you want to go even deeper, check out Beyond Fear, an intensive 12-module workshop on overcoming your fears and kicking even more butt! To learn more, check it out here:

http://beyond-fear.com

Or, if you want one-on-one help, you can check out my email coaching program here:

http://17000-days.com/clarity/

ABOUT THE AUTHOR

I'm Cara Stein. I've always wanted to be a writer, but I took a roundabout way of getting here. Among other relics of career change and self-reinvention, I have a PhD in computer science, assorted programming skills, several years' teaching experience, and advanced skills in wasting a whole afternoon surfing the internet.

When I wrote this book, getting unstuck and overcoming fears had been my chief occupations for a few years, between career change and completely remodeling my life. Then I started my own business and quit my job. When I experienced how much easier it all is than it looks, I realized I had to spread the word.

I'm the founder of 17,000 Days, a blog about remembering that life is short and making your best days a common occurrence. Whether you're stuck, lost, or just looking to enjoy your life more, I've been there! I can provide advice, guidance, and vision. I'm a big believer in self-reinvention and sculpting your life into what you want it to be. I love guiding people to do the same.

My other books include *How to be Happy (No Fairy Dust or Moonbeams Required)* and *Reclaim Your Love: How to Fix Your*

Relationship. My latest project is a coloring book for adults called *Relax and Color.* That book was a pure passion project for me. I never thought I could be an artist, but designing my own coloring book showed me that I can.

In addition to working on my own books, I help other people finish and publish their books. I do the whole process, from writing and editing to design and layout. It's a lot of fun—getting to work with books all the time is a dream job for me.

I live in Huntsville, Alabama, with one stripy gray kitty cat.

Notes

[1] eDrugRehab. "Why children of addicts marry other addicts." http://www.edrugrehab.com/why-children-of-addictsmarry-other-addicts.html

[2] Susan Jeffers. Feel the fear and do it anyway. Fawcett Columbine, New York, 1987.

[3] Albert Ellis and Arthur Lange. How to keep people from pushing your buttons. Birch Lane Press, New York, 1994, p. 63.

[4] Martin Seligman. Authentic Happiness. Free Press, New York, 2002.

[5] Mira Kirshenbaum. The Emotional Energy Factor: the secrets high-energy people use to beat emotional fatigue. Delta, New York, 2004.

[6] David D. Burns. Feeling Good. Avon, New York, 1980, pp. 32-43.

[7] Albert Ellis and Arthur Lange. How to keep people from pushing your buttons. Birch Lane Press, New York, 1994, p. 63.

[8] Timothy Ferriss. The 4-Hour Workweek. Crown Publishers, New York, 2007, p. 117.

[9] Time-Life Books. Library of curious and unusual facts: inventive genius. Time-Life Education, Virginia, 1991, p. 97. Cited on http://www.snopes.com/business/origins/post-it.aspemb

[10] Pauline Rose Clance. The Impostor Phenomenon. Peachtree Publishers, Atlanta, GA, 1985. pp. 26-28.

[11,12] David Rock. Your Brain at work. Harper Business, New York, 2009.

[13] Drew Emborsky. "Is THAT what rain looks like?" No longer available; formerly located at: http://blog.thecrochetdude.com/2008/06/23/is-that-what-rain-looks-like.aspx

[14] Marci Shimoff with Carol Kline. Happy for no reason. Free Press, New York, 2008, p. 84.

[15] Claire E. Adams and Mark R. Leary. "Promoting self-compassionate attitudes toward eating among restrictive and guilty eaters." Journal of Social and Clinical Psychology, vol. 26, No. 10 (2007), pp. 1120-1144. Available at http://self-compassion.org/wp-content/uploads/publications/AdamsLearyeating_attitudes.pdf

[16] Martha Beck. "When and how to say 'enough!'" O, The Oprah Magazine, April 2009. Available at http://www.oprah.com/spirit/Martha-Becks-Strategy-to-Lower-Stress-and-Improve-Your-Life/be

[17] John Ratey with Eric Hagerman. Spark: The revolutionary new science of exercise and the brain. Little, Brown and Company, New York, 2008.

[18] Lewis Carroll. Alice's Adventures in Wonderland, Chapter 6. Cited at Lenny's Alice in Wonderland Site. http://www.alice-in-wonderland.net/alice3.html

[19] Walter Anderson. The Confidence Course. HarperCollins, New York, 1997, p. 183.

[20] Cal Newport. "The Minimalist's Guide to cultivating Passion." Guest post on Zen Habits. Http://zenhabits.net/cultivating-passion/

[21,22] Hyrum W. Smith. 10 Natural laws of successful time and life management. Warner Books, New York, 1994, pp 56-57.

[23,24,25,26] John P. Strelecky and Tim Brownson. How to be Rich and Happy. PDF version, p. 32; 81,82. Available at http://howtoberichandhappy.com/

[27] Charlie Gilkey and Jonathan Mead. The Dojo. Self-published, no longer available.

[28] Jonathan Mead. "The limit erasing technique." No longer available. See http://paidtoexist.com/limiting-belief-erasing-technique/

[29] Lachlan Cotter. "How to change your world, Part 2: choosing to be free." http://www.theartofaudacity.com/choosing-freedom/

[30] Karol Gajda. Mind Control Method. p. 20. Self-published, no longer available.

[31] Karen Walrond. "The Beauty of Different." World Domination Summit, Portland, OR, June 4, 2011.

[32] Jonathan Mead. Reclaiming Your Dreams, p. 45. Available at http://www.illuminatedmind.net/reclaim-your-dreams/

[33] Mars Dorian. "How 'bridging' took my entrepreneur friend from poor and shitty to grrreat and successful." http://www.marsdorian.com/2011/04/the-power-of-bridging/

[34] Seth Godin. The Dip. Portfolio, New York, 2007.

[35] Allen Fine with Rebecca R. Merrill. You already know how to be great. Portfolio/Penguin, New York, 2010, pp. 52-63.

[36] Mihaly Csikszentmihalyi. Finding Flow. Basic Books, New York, 1997.

[37,38,39] Neil Fiore. The Now Habit. Jeremy P. Tarcher/Putnam, New York, 1989.

[40] Steve Jobs. Commencement address to Stanford University, delivered June 12, 2005. http://news.stanford.edu/news/2005/june15/jobs-061505.html

www.ingramcontent.com/pod-product-compliance
Lightning Source LLC
Chambersburg PA
CBHW052000090426
42741CB00008B/1481